From Nowhere

JAMIE
VARDY
From Nowhere MY STORY

WITH STUART JAMES

EBURY
PRESS

3 5 7 9 10 8 6 4

Ebury Press, an imprint of Ebury Publishing
20 Vauxhall Bridge Road
London SW1V 2SA

Ebury Press is part of the Penguin Random House group of companies
whose addresses can be found at global.penguinrandomhouse.com

Penguin
Random House
UK

First published by Ebury Press in 2016
This edition published in 2017

www.penguin.co.uk

A CIP catalogue record for this book is available from the British Library

ISBN 9781785034848

Printed and bound in Great Britain by Clays Ltd, St Ives PLC

Penguin Random House is committed to a sustainable
future for our business, our readers and our planet.
This book is made from Forest Stewardship Council®
certified paper.

CONTENTS

PROLOGUE

'JAMIE VARDY'S HAVING A PARTY'

I reached into the thin blue carrier bag, pulled out the first can of Stella and cracked it open. It was 11am on Bank Holiday Monday, the streets around Leicester city centre were quiet and for the next seven hours a needle loaded with ink was going to be jamming into my ribs, stomach, hips and back. A four-pack was my anaesthetic.

There was a closed sign in the window of Blue Ink Tattoo Studio on Belgrave Gate, but they'd agreed to open for a private appointment I'd been trying to organise for weeks. The owner had a day off after scoring the equaliser at Manchester United 24 hours earlier, but Wes Morgan's staff made me feel right at home as I sipped on the beer they'd picked up for me from the off licence around the corner.

A couple of passers-by did a double take as they glanced through the window and saw me perched on a stool in the reception area, running my eyes over the pocket-watch design that had been drawn up to mark the birth of my daughter, Sofia. I couldn't help thinking that it looked a touch more professional than my first tattoo, which was done in someone's living room in Sheffield and cost me £25.

I took off my T-shirt and walked into one of the treatment rooms, set up my iPad on a little table and watched three live matches – Walsall v Fleetwood, Brighton v Derby and Burnley v QPR – back-to-back, grimacing and wincing as my skin sweated blood.

There was one more game to tune into later in the day, but I needed to be out of the tattooist's chair and at home when that kicked off. It was Chelsea v Tottenham Hotspur at Stamford Bridge, and by the time Christian Fuchs and Robert Huth picked me up just after 6pm to head back to Melton Mowbray, the internet was rife with reports that 'Jamie Vardy's having a party'. So much for the plan we'd made at Old Trafford to keep things secret.

Wes was on the phone to me in the afternoon, more interested in discussing the arrangements for later than receiving an update on my tattoo. The captain wanted to make sure that every player was comfortable with Leicester's media team coming along to film and photograph any title-winning celebrations should Tottenham fail to beat Chelsea. In the end, we agreed to let a few of them attend a party that may as well have been advertised on flyers, because there were that many people camped outside my home and craning their necks to look over the boundary wall.

Inside the house, half-a-dozen lads were scattered around the television screen in the kitchen, while the rest set up camp in the snug room as bottles of beer were passed around, along with the odd glass of whiskey to calm the nerves. I was lying on the floor, eating nibbles and trying to get into a position where my tattoo would cause me the least discomfort.

Everybody was chilled and relaxed – until kick-off. Then we put our Chelsea shirts on and may as well have been sitting in a city-centre pub as we screamed at the TV, 'Send him off, ref!' after any Spurs foul. Every swear word under the sun came out as Harry Kane rounded Asmir Begovic to open the scoring, and when Spurs doubled their lead just before half-time it killed the atmosphere dead. 'Well, this was worth sorting out,' I said to Wes.

It had turned into no more than a Bank Holiday piss-up for the lads, and we could all imagine the headlines the next day about Tottenham spoiling our party, complete with photos of 'glum-faced' players leaving my house. Chelsea looked dead and buried, and our minds were already turning to the home game against Everton on Saturday. 'We'll just have to finish the job then,' said a few of the lads, trying to raise spirits.

Yet just before the hour mark, everything changed. Willian took a corner and Gary Cahill beat Hugo Lloris with a left-foot shot that transformed the mood. 'Fucking get in!'

All of a sudden it was game on. We weren't just Chelsea supporters any more, we were playing for Guus Hiddink's team – trying to touch home Eden Hazard's low cross at one end and block Christian Eriksen's shot at the other.

Then it happened.

Hazard picked up the ball wide on the left, wriggled past a couple of players, rolled a pass into Diego Costa, got it back and … f–u–c–k–i–n–g h–e–l–l. With one fantastic swing of his right boot, the Chelsea number 10 curled the ball into the top corner and Melton Mowbray had lift off.

People were running everywhere. Riyad Mahrez and Matty James skipped through a stair-gate to join a pile of bodies hugging one another, I took the shortcut and somersaulted from the kitchen to the sofa in the snug room – a move not seen since I scored on the opening day against Sunderland – and Marcin Wasilewski was dragging Wes around the kitchen by his ankles. It was pandemonium.

With only seven minutes remaining everybody congregated in the kitchen, where the media team were frantically setting up their equipment. We were within touching distance of the

TV as well as the title, standing shoulder to shoulder with one another and not daring to take our eyes off the screen as we counted down the seconds.

It was like getting ready for Big Ben to chime midnight on New Year's Eve – except that occurs every 12 months. Leicester winning the title hadn't happened in 132 years. Six minutes of injury time were up and the clock was edging towards 97 minutes when Willian played the ball out to Hazard, who took a touch before the final whistle sounded. Referee Mark Clattenburg must have blown three times but we only heard it once.

The room just erupted. It was crazy. We were lost in the moment, going completely wild as we danced around the kitchen, screaming and shouting, embracing and clinging onto one another. A camera was flashing, people were bouncing off walls, the TV went on the blink and we started singing, 'Championes! Championes! Olé! Olé! Olé!'

I couldn't take it in and nor could anyone else. One of the lads was in tears while another just kept shaking his head. Outside, a couple of the players were having a quiet moment to themselves on the steps down to the garden, where the lawn looked more like a prison exercise yard as people paced up and down. A few were on the phone to wives and friends, others were just trying to make sense of it all.

But nothing made sense. Not when the final whistle blew and not when I went to bed six-and-a-half hours later. Leicester City – relegation favourites and 5,000-1 title outsiders – were the Premier League champions.

1

BLUE-AND-WHITE
STRIPES

David Hirst. I didn't want to be anybody else. Once I had a ball at my feet, which was every spare moment of the day, I became the legend who played up front for the club I loved.

I idolised David Hirst because he did exactly what I wanted to do – score goals for Sheffield Wednesday. Only he did it better than anyone I'd ever seen. Left foot, right foot, headers, tap-ins, volleys, thunderbolts – you name it, Hirst scored them. Just as I did when I recreated all those goals, complete with running commentary, in my back garden in Malin Bridge, or in the pub car park across the road, where a climbing frame outside the Yew Tree Inn doubled up as a goal. David Hirst might not have known it, but he was every bit as prolific on that little area of concrete as he was at Hillsborough.

My parents lived across the street from the pub, in a three-bedroom semi-detached house on Loxley Road that we moved into towards the end of my time at Malin Bridge Primary School. I'd often kick about in the car park until it was dark, playing the game 'Wembley' and trying to get a goal that counted double by shooting the ball through a couple of triangles that were conveniently positioned in the top corners of the climbing frame.

Ashley Cross, who lived a couple of streets away and went to the same school as me, would usually be one of the dozen or so lads joining in, along with Tim Stanton and his brother Ben, who went on to be a guitarist in an indie band called Harrisons – named after Harrison Road, which was a stone's throw away from the pub.

I'd nearly always have my blue-and-white striped Wednesday kit on, reliving the games I'd watched at Hillsborough, which was less than two miles away from our house, dominating the area as well as my childhood.

My dad first started taking me to Hillsborough when I was around the age of five, and we'd be on the Kop, which was one of the biggest single-tier stands in Europe. There was room for about 20,000 people – I didn't even know there were that many Wednesday fans – on a huge banked terrace that seemed to go on for ever. As I was so little I'd get lifted up onto one of the blue handrails and nothing could beat that view. It was like looking out on a field of dreams as I watched John Sheridan, John Harkes and Nigel Pearson playing for a Wednesday team that finished third in the old First Division in 1992.

I loved the atmosphere, the singing and the roar when Wednesday scored. But most of all I loved the striker everybody called 'Hirsty'. The Wednesday number 9 had a left foot like a rocket – his 114 miles per hour volley that nearly broke the crossbar at Highbury in 1996 was recorded as the fastest shot in Premier League history – and whenever he got the ball, you could feel the excitement. I expected something to happen and so did everyone around me.

Sir Alex Ferguson kept trying to sign him for Manchester United, but Hirsty spent more than a decade at Hillsborough. Wednesday felt like *his* club, just like it was my club, and when he pulled on that famous jersey he played as if his life depended on it. I remember him breaking his ankle against Arsenal and not only getting up and carrying on, but scoring an absolute wonder goal – a scissor kick in August 1992 with that brilliant left foot. Lying face down on the turf afterwards, he was unable to move, never mind celebrate.

My obsession with David Hirst, Sheffield Wednesday and football probably didn't help my schoolwork, and it certainly caused a few problems with our neighbours. In fact, more than 20 years later, I've got a confession to make to the miserable woman who lived next door to us on Holme Lane, which is also in Malin Bridge.

There were four houses in a row, with a communal garden running behind, and I knew that our neighbour didn't like me kicking a ball on the strip of grass that we all shared. Actually, that's an understatement. She absolutely hated it and never stopped moaning. So much so that she took it upon herself to pop all my footballs. You've got to be a bloody mean person to do that to a child.

So when I saw that a window had been delivered one day and left out the back of her house, it was a chance to get even. The window, she later discovered, was smashed before the glaziers had a chance to put it in. What nobody knew until now is that I was the guilty party and had put a brick through it.

It wasn't a very nice thing to do, admittedly, and I'd have been in major trouble at home if my parents had found out. But the way I looked at it was that stopping me from playing football was a much bigger crime because it was all I'd ever wanted to do from the moment I could walk.

• • •

Born on 11 January 1987, I spent the first few years of my life on Overton Road, growing up in the shadows of Hillsborough stadium. The house belonged to my nan and granddad, Mavis and Gerald Clewes, and the narrow, covered walkway that led to the back garden was a perfect place to kick a ball because I could strike it against the gate at the other end and it would keep coming back to me.

Although I started at Marlcliffe Primary School, it wasn't long before we moved into the property on Holme Lane and I changed schools, to Malin Bridge. A few years later we moved to the house on Loxley Road, only a five-minute walk away.

I lived with my younger sister Lauren and my parents. My mum, Lisa, worked for a solicitors' and my dad, Phil, had quite a few jobs. He was a joiner and later became a driving instructor, before going on to operate tower cranes. I remained close to my grandparents, who'd sometimes take me away on holiday to Great Yarmouth or Skegness, where we'd play crazy golf and have a bit of fun.

It was a working-class upbringing and we weren't blessed with lots of money, but I never wanted much, and when it came to the few things that really mattered to me – like a Wednesday shirt or a new pair of football boots – my parents wouldn't think twice.

I felt happy and settled in Malin Bridge, which is a suburb about two-and-a-half miles from Sheffield's city centre. It was a close-knit community and the area's industrial history was everywhere you looked, from the old corn mill on the banks of the River Loxley to the La Plata Works on Holme Lane, which was home to Burgon & Ball, the famous Sheffield steelmakers who'd been operating from there ever since the end of the nineteenth century.

Some days I'd go fishing on the river with my dad or granddad, but most of the time I was on one of the backstreets kicking a ball with anyone who fancied a game. There was a red-fronted garage on Cotswold Road that used to take a bit of a hammering. When one of the residents came out and moved us on, we'd sometimes play around the corner, on the crossroads where Chiltern Road meets Leslie Road. Hardly any traffic passed through and a neatly kept hedge made a good goal. That was my life – football, football, football.

At Malin Bridge Primary School I'd sit in the classroom staring out of the window in between watching the hands on the clock go round, hoping and praying for break-time so that I could get into the yard and have a kickabout with my friends.

Only one thing interested me at school other than football, and that was Mr Pemberton's maths lessons. With every other subject I went through the motions, thinking far more about Wednesday's next game or the goal I was going to score in the playground. But when Mr Pemberton stood at the front of the classroom he had my undivided attention for as long as he wanted. That's because he was a brilliant teacher and a lovely man – he even had some sweets named after him in the local newsagents – and maths was my favourite subject by a mile.

In fact, outside of football, Mr Pemberton's times-tables tests at junior school were the highlight of my week.

He used to draw a clock on the board, with the numbers one to twelve, and then he'd put a number in the middle. Each person would then take it in turns to stand at the front, where the pressure was on. Mr Pemberton would say, 'Right, 30 seconds, starting now.' He would point his cane at one of the numbers on the clock and you had to multiply it by the number in the middle. I absolutely loved it and, unlike most other academic work at school, I was really good at it.

I don't know where this natural aptitude for numbers came from – maybe the time spent in the pub as a kid, where I'd often be in the games room, either with my parents or a friend's dad, adding up scores and breaks on the snooker table or calculating checkouts while playing darts. Going through all the potential permutations of Saturday's results and predicting where Wednesday were going to be in the league table probably helped as well.

• • •

The early nineties was a great time to be a Wednesday fan because they were enjoying a golden era in which they'd emerged as one of the top clubs in English football. In 1991 they beat Manchester United to win the League Cup, there was that third-place finish the following season, and in 1993, when I was six, they visited Wembley four times in the space of seven weeks.

The first of those games was the only thing that anybody in the area was talking about at the time because it was an FA Cup semi-final against Sheffield United, our bitter rivals. Wednesday won 2–1 in extra-time, and the highlight of the day, without doubt, was Chris Waddle opening the scoring after only two minutes with a 30-yard free-kick. 'Alan Kelly beaten before he's touched the ball!' Barry Davies said – I would watch the *Road to Wembley* video so much that I'd learnt the commentary off by heart – as Waddle swept a curling left-foot shot inside the United goalkeeper's near post. Wowzers. I loved that goal.

Unfortunately, that was the only match Wednesday won out of the four at Wembley. We lost 2–1 against Arsenal in the League Cup final, when Steve Morrow broke his arm in the post-match celebrations after Tony Adams tried to pick him up but dropped him.

Arsenal also got the better of us in the FA Cup final in a replay, which I went along to after skiving off school for the afternoon. The match was played on a Thursday night, and I think my mum made up an excuse and said that I had a dental appointment, just so we could get from Sheffield to London in time. Not that I knew much about the journey – I fell asleep in the car and woke up at Wembley. It turned into a really long evening because the kick-off was delayed for half an hour due to a bad accident on the motorway, and the game also ended up going to extra-time.

Chris Waddle equalised after Ian Wright put Arsenal in front, and it looked like it was going to be the first FA Cup final to be decided by penalties. But in the 119th minute Andy Linighan broke my heart when he met a corner with a thumping header that Chris Woods got his hands to but was unable to keep out. To cap it all, it pissed it down all night and, as we had seats in the front row, we were wet through come the end. Welcome to life as a Wednesday supporter.

Yet I kept coming back for more and barely missed a game at Hillsborough. I'd often queue up for autographs – especially Hirsty's – and I always looked forward to the final home game of the season because it was a chance to run on to the pitch and try to get a shirt or a free pair of boots from one of the players.

As I got a bit older I came to realise that one of the other benefits of being inside a football stadium as a child was that I could get away with the sort of behaviour that wouldn't be tolerated anywhere else. In particular, dishing out a few swear words. As long as I didn't repeat them at home I was on safe ground.

• • •

Emulating my heroes in the playground was starting to pay off. I went along to Hillsborough Leisure Centre for some basic coaching sessions for kids, and later joined a local junior side called York County. Small, slight and quick, I played up front and scored four or five goals in most games. I also struck up what would become a lifelong friendship with a lad called Ian Collins, who was the right-back.

The first major transfer of my career took place at around the age of ten, when I swapped York County for Sheffield Rangers. My dad knew David Mace, the Sheffield Rangers manager, because he was also a driving instructor, and I'd crossed paths with his son Daniel before. Daniel, in my eyes, had it made because he was already on Wednesday's books.

Sheffield Rangers was a step up in standard. The club had a good reputation in the area and some of the people involved had links with Wednesday, including David, who did some coaching there, so playing for them felt like a good decision all round. Chirpy lad that I was, I quickly settled in, and it wasn't long before I got the invitation that made me feel like all my Christmases had come at once.

Wednesday wanted me to go for a trial at Middlewood, their training ground in Hillsborough. Clive Baker was Wednesday's academy director at the time – he had a long history with the club, stretching back to 1984 – and I must have made a good impression over a few training sessions because they were happy to give me a place. In my mind, life couldn't get any better, and to top it all I even got two complimentary tickets for the South Stand, close to the Kop, to watch them every week.

Training took place at Middlewood for two hours every Monday, Tuesday and Thursday nights, and I was always early because I couldn't wait to get started. If Wednesday were at home on the Saturday, I'd go along with my dad to watch them, and then on the Sunday I'd play for the club's schoolboy teams against other professional sides, generally in the north and as far afield as Newcastle. In short, Sheffield Wednesday had completely taken over my life.

The only negative thing about it all was that I couldn't play any competitive matches away from Wednesday because I was now committed to the club. Street football, however, carried on, whether in Malin Bridge or Hillsborough, where my cousin lived. Sometimes a few of us would get on our bikes and cycle down to the stadium, where we'd play outside the Leppings Lane End, using the big blue exit doors behind the stand as a goal. One day Clive strolled by for a meeting at the stadium and did a double take as he saw me with my mates, booting the ball around. 'So you're the reason why we're always having to repaint these doors!' he said, with a smile.

I told Clive that we didn't have anywhere else to play, but it was more a case that none of us could get enough of

Wednesday. We all dreamed of following in the footsteps of our heroes by playing at Hillsborough, and one afternoon, in a deserted stadium, that wish briefly came true.

During those kickabouts outside the stadium, the ball would often go over the top of the perimeter wall, so rather than find security, we'd scale the fence to get it. On this occasion we were feeling a bit mischievous and decided to not just climb over but to head down to the pitch. We were having a great time, passing the ball around in front of 40,000 empty seats, taking it in turns to be David Hirst and Paolo Di Canio – and then a security guard suddenly started shouting at us, so we all scarpered.

Di Canio signed for Wednesday in 1997, a year after Benito Carbone joined the club, and I had one of the best experiences of my childhood with the maverick Italian pair.

We were in for training at Middlewood on a Saturday morning and the first team didn't have a match, so the players were just doing a light session. I was knocking a ball about with another lad from my age group and, completely out of the blue, Carbone and Di Canio challenged us to a game of head tennis.

At that time they were probably the best players at Wednesday – both were record signings for the club when they joined – so it was the stuff of dreams to be asked to take them on. It was also the stuff of nightmares once the head tennis started – they absolutely pasted us.

On one side of the net were two kids just trying to make sure that they could get the ball back any way possible, often without a lot of finesse; on the other side Carbone and Di Canio were flicking it up, doing bicycle kicks and turning it into an exhibition. All I could do was think, Wow.

I loved Di Canio. What a player. So much passion, so much talent. But mention Di Canio and Sheffield Wednesday and everybody thinks of one incident – when he pushed over referee Paul Alcock after getting sent off in a game against Arsenal in September 1998. Two things made me smile about that, the first being the theatrical way that the referee went down – it seemed to take him half a minute to fall to the floor – and the second was that comedy moment when Nigel Winterburn came over to have a go and then shat himself when Di Canio motioned to do something to him.

• • •

I'd not long started at Wisewood Secondary School when Di Canio got his 11-match ban, and I also found myself in a spot of bother. I sat down for registration in my tutor group on my first day and, before I'd had the chance to take my pencil case out of my bag, the teacher said, 'Can Jamie Vardy go to the head teacher's office.' It turned out that someone had been throwing stones at the windows of my old primary school in Malin Bridge, and for some reason I was the chief suspect.

I explained to Mr Barr, the head teacher, that it was nothing to do with me, which was true, but I knew that it was a black mark against my name.

In truth, education was no more important to me at Wise-wood than it had been at primary school. If anything, the balance had tipped even more in favour of football, because once I signed for Wednesday everything was mapped out in front of me – I was going to be a professional footballer with my hometown club.

I'd walk to school every morning thinking about it, stopping off at Beth's Buttery & Cafe on Dykes Lane, where I'd spend 20 pence on bread and dripping – which is basically just fat in a sandwich and probably one of the most unhealthy things you can eat – ahead of another day of boredom.

Pretty much the only time I came alive at school was on the field at break-time, when I'd be more than happy to join in a football match with the oldest kids, and during PE lessons. I loved taking part in any sport and was particularly good at track and field. If we had an athletics championship at school, I would go in for the 1,500 metres as well as the 200- and 100-metre sprints, because although I was fast, I had stamina too. I was also capable of a decent leap, so despite being tiny I'd represent the school at the high jump.

In years 7, 8 and 9, which is ages 11 to 14, we weren't allowed to throw the javelin at school because it was considered too dangerous, so we had to use a cricket ball instead. The principle was the same – take a run up and throw it as far as you can. One teacher would watch to make sure that you didn't put your foot over the line, and another would be out in the field to mark where the ball landed. When it came to my turn on sports day I was convinced that I'd throw it a lot further than the teacher out in the field was expecting.

'I think you need to tell him to go and stand further back,' I said to the teacher monitoring the line.

'No, he's fine where he is,' he replied.

'But I'll throw it further than that,' I said.

'I'm sure you won't,' said the teacher.

I sprinted up to the line and launched it, and I'll never forget the sight of the teacher in the field watching the cricket ball sail over him and then frantically running to try to get near to where it landed. I think I held the record for a long time after I left – something like 77 metres – and in fact it may not ever have been broken because the school isn't there any more. It was knocked down and replaced with a sports centre a few years ago.

My running ability just seemed to come naturally. We went on an Army residential course while at school, where we stayed in barracks and got a taste of what it was like to be in the military. They would wake us up early to do an assault course, a bit of archery and the official Army bleep test, which

I did well at. People were dropping out either side of me and for quite a while I was running on my own. But I also got a bollocking – the story of my life.

We were doing the test in a sports hall that had no air-conditioning and it was like a furnace in there. I got to level 12, and although I had plenty left in my legs, I was burning up, so I whipped my top off and carried on bare-chested.

'Get your top back on now!' shouted the sergeant in a booming voice.

I was determined not to stop running, so I kept going while also trying to get my top the right way around and back over my head. As any bloke will know, doing two things at once is beyond us, and I ended up getting in one hell of a tangle, still running full pelt and barely able to see.

'Just forget it!' barked the sergeant.

I carried on without the shirt and did another level and a half.

• • •

I was willing to have a go at anything physical. I even went to a few boxing classes, not because I wanted to fight, but it was just another sport for me to try.

Frau Drew must have wished that I had the same enthusiasm for learning German, but unfortunately for her that wasn't the case. I don't think it ever got beyond '*Ich heisse* Jamie

Vardy', probably because I was rarely in the classroom. She would turn up and send me out straight away, usually because I'd been talking when I should have been listening. So I'd sit at a single table in the corridor, with only a German textbook to keep me company.

Looking back, I was probably a bit of a pain to a few teachers at secondary school, especially in my last couple of years. I just don't think there was the interest or motivation to push myself in the classroom because I'd been with Wednesday for so long that I couldn't imagine a future without football.

All the feedback from the club seemed to be positive. You'd receive an update on how you were progressing at Christmas, and at the end of the season you'd find out whether you were being kept on or not. Some lads drifted away, but I was always one of those retained and my reports were decent.

Ben Wilkinson, son of Howard, the former Wednesday and Leeds United manager, was in my age group at the club and so was a guy called Danny Care, who played in the same positions as me – on either wing or up front – and was of a not dissimilar size. We were both little for our age.

Everybody develops at different rates physically, but I just didn't seem to get much taller and I certainly didn't fill out. Some of the lads I'd come up against were huge in comparison. Derby County's Under-15 team had Tom Huddlestone in the side. He's only two weeks older than me but he was built like a man then. Tom was playing for the reserves at 15 and the first team at 16, which would have been unthinkable for me.

By the time I turned 15, in January 2002, Sheffield Wednesday were in a mess. The glorious days at the start of the nineties, when David Hirst was on fire and the club were challenging for silverware under Ron Atkinson and Trevor Francis, felt like a lifetime ago.

Wednesday had been relegated from the Premier League in 2000, with manager Danny Wilson sacked towards the end of that season. Paul Jewell lasted only eight months in charge and Peter Shreeves, his replacement, was gone after a similar period of time. On top of that, the club was in huge debt.

Closer to home, Clive had stepped down as academy director in 2001, as part of a major overhaul of the youth set-up. Jimmy Shoulder, who was the Wales Under-21 manager, took over and brought in several of his own staff. Not the sort to let things trouble me, I just got on with it and backed myself to keep doing what I'd done from day one at Middlewood – prove I was good enough.

At school I was being encouraged to explore other options. There was an outreach programme being rolled out at the time to open up university opportunities for kids who may not otherwise get the chance. I was one of those selected, and one weekend I went along to the University of Sheffield with some other pupils from Wisewood. We stayed in the halls, did various activities during the day and went to a disco they'd put on for everyone in the evening. But I didn't want to be there one bit, and the experience did nothing to alter my view that the only thing that interested me was becoming a professional footballer for Sheffield Wednesday.

I felt I had all the attributes. Although I was naturally right-footed, I was more than capable of using my left because I had always practised with both as a kid. I had an eye for goal and was blessed with speed which, together with my aggression, made up for the fact that I was the smallest player in the team at a touch under five-foot tall. At least, that's how I saw things.

Wednesday came to a different conclusion. I tried so hard to erase this day from my mind in the weeks, months and years afterwards that I can't tell you who broke it to me that I 'wasn't big enough' to make it as a footballer. It could have been Jimmy Shoulder or Jim Hinch, my Under-16 manager, or someone else at the academy – I'm just not sure who made the decision. All I know is that I walked out of Wednesday absolutely devastated. I'd supported the club all my life, and now they were telling me that they didn't want me around any more – that they didn't think I had what it took to wear that shirt.

If I remember right, there was some talk in the meeting about the age group above being abolished, so I'd have to jump up several years and the academy coaches thought that

I didn't have the physical stature to cope. But I wasn't really listening by that point. Once I knew that they were cutting me loose, not much registered.

I was distraught. Anger and confusion were bubbling up inside. Everything I'd ever wanted had just been snatched away from me. Nothing made sense as I turned things over in my mind, wondering why they couldn't give me more time to develop physically, whether it would have been different if Clive had still been academy director.

But dwelling on what might have been wasn't going to help me going forward. And that was what worried me most – the future. Reality dawned on me as I thought, *Shit, I've not tried in school for the past two years. What the hell is going to happen next?*

I sat my exams that summer and ended up with one GCSE at grade C and above. No prizes for guessing the subject – maths. Everything else had passed me by, just like my childhood. Three evenings a week at Sheffield Wednesday, every Sunday travelling all over the north of England, and I had fuck all to show for it.

Disillusioned and dejected, I went back to where it all started and played a few games for York County, not far from where I lived but a million miles away from where I wanted to be. My mate Ian Collins was still with the club and I started to do a bit of fishing with him on a weekend. He'd joined an angling club called Mercury Taxis and travelled all over Yorkshire to compete in a league. I was nothing like as good as him at fishing but that didn't matter. In fact, nothing seemed to matter any more as my boots gathered dust and all thoughts of becoming the next David Hirst disappeared from my mind.

2

'HE'D BETTER BE GOOD
IN THOSE BOOTS'

'And the winner is … Jamie Vardy.'

Just when I needed to see my name on the notice board at Stocksbridge Park Steels, it had a funny knack of appearing. I was usually short of money and well behind on my £3.50 subs, so it was always welcome news to find out that I'd won the £100 top prize in the '500 club' raffle. Everybody had to pay £3.50 a week to play for Stocksbridge, even if they were getting a wage as one of the first team, but being a member of the '500 club' had its perks now and again. It raised about £10,000 a year for Stocksbridge and occasionally put a bit of money in a player's pocket. The fact that I tended to owe the club a few quid whenever I got lucky made me suspicious that the draw was rigged, but I wasn't complaining.

I didn't know a thing about Stocksbridge Park Steels before I signed, and I think most people's first impression when they go there is that it's an unlikely place to find a football ground. For those who have never paid a visit to that part of the world, Stocksbridge is a steel town on the edge of the Peak District, in South Yorkshire, only a few miles from where I grew up in Malin Bridge.

When you drive through Stocksbridge and turn off the main road onto Nanny Hill, past the old clock tower on the left and onto Bocking Hill, it's so steep that it's as much as you can do to get the car out of second gear. Eventually it runs into Bracken Moor Lane, where the road continues to climb until you can see the ground over the top of the stone wall on the left. It's still the same 450-seater main stand there today as when I played for the club – the only difference being that they've now named it after me.

The first time I went along to Bracken Moor, on a Thursday night with my dad some time near the end of 2003, I wasn't sure what to expect or even if I was doing the right thing. I'd been playing for Wickersley Youth, in Rotherham, alongside a lad called Matthew Burton, who had also been released by Wednesday a bit before me. We went to Thomas Rotherham College together, where I studied something to do with sports science, and Matt talked me into 'getting back into it' and turning out for Wickersley on a Sunday morning. We played at Wickersley Secondary School and trained on a Thursday evening at Herringthorpe Leisure Centre in Rotherham, which was a little way from home in Sheffield, so I'd often stay over at Matt's parents' house and go straight to college from there on a Friday.

One week I played against Stocksbridge Under-18s, did OK and Steve Adams, their manager, found out that I lived locally and also knew one of his players. Steve rang me up a few days later and asked whether I would be interested in joining Stocksbridge. He probably expected me to jump at the chance – Stocksbridge were a proper non-league club – but I wasn't sure. I didn't like the idea of letting Matt down. He was a mate and I hadn't been with Wickersley for that long, so it seemed wrong to walk away. But Steve persevered, and eventually I agreed to meet up for a chat, watch a bit of training and have a look at their facilities.

Stocksbridge's first team were playing in the Northern Premier League Division One, which was effectively the eighth tier of English football. They had a reserve side as well as a youth team, so it felt like quite a professional set-up. There was a chance to move up step by step, and I liked the sound of that. It meant that I wouldn't have to go to another club and start all over again when I was too old for the Under-18s.

The pitch was very good for that level, but there was a downside. With the ground being so high up, it was open to the elements and, as a result, fucking freezing in the winter. If it snowed an inch in Hillsborough, it was a foot deep in Stocksbridge, so lots of matches were postponed and there'd be a backlog of fixtures at the end of the season. Also, it was a nightmare when there was a bit of wind, because it would blow a gale at the Bracken Moor ground. I played in matches where the keeper would kick the ball out and watch the wind carry it straight back to him. When the fog came in, it was like a blanket over the pitch. In one match against Kidsgrove you couldn't see either goal when you were stood on the halfway line. When we scored, half a dozen of our players claimed they'd got the final touch.

After agreeing to sign for Stocksbridge, I went into their Under-18 team, who played on a Sunday morning on a pitch across the road from the main ground. I say a pitch, it was more like a field, but that was fine with me. I just wanted to kick a ball and get a smile back on my face. There certainly wasn't any bigger picture – the idea of trying to be a professional footballer wasn't in my head at all. My confidence was shot to bits after being released by Wednesday, and I didn't think about proving people wrong. I just thought about playing for Stocksbridge Under-18s.

I scored plenty of goals, finishing as the second-highest scorer in my first season and top scorer the following year, which did wonders for me, and pretty soon I was Jack the Lad in the dressing room, always keen to be the one to get the glory. I played in a cup semi-final against Handsworth, our local rivals, that went to extra-time and penalties. Steve was scribbling down the names of the penalty takers, and I asked him if I could take the fifth and final spot-kick. I had a picture in my mind of it being the winning penalty and, getting a bit ahead of myself, told Steve that I was going to slide on my knees in front of their fans after I scored. As it happened, I needed to score to keep us in it, and Steve said that the penalty I took was one of the worst he'd ever seen – way off target and in need of a search party to look for the ball at the bottom of Nanny Hill. It was good to have my confidence back, at least – even if it was sometimes misplaced.

Twelve months later, I took another penalty for Stocksbridge in a shoot-out, this time for the reserves against Athersley Recreation in another cup semi-final. I can remember it clearly because Geoff Horsfield, the former Fulham, Birmingham and West Brom striker, used to play for Athersley, and before the game people were talking about how he'd made a donation to the club to help improve their facilities. Anyway, I missed my kick again – this time it was on target but the keeper just managed to save it – but the referee said he'd moved off his line, so I had to retake it. As I put the ball on the spot, their keeper said to me, 'You're not going to go the same way.'

You cheeky bastard, I thought. I put it in exactly the same place, only this time it went past him and I ran off celebrating.

• • •

By the end of my second season at Stocksbridge I was good enough to be playing in Steve Shutt's reserve team on a Saturday as well as the Under-18s on a Sunday. I couldn't get enough of football, but I certainly didn't feel the same way about academic work. After a year at Thomas Rotherham College I should have been at Barnsley College for another 12 months, on another sport-related course, but I stopped attending. It wasn't that I couldn't do the work. I just didn't want to, so my grades were horrendous. I ended up getting a BTEC from one of the colleges but I really don't know how.

I only turned up for as long as I did because there was a chance to play football against other colleges. In one game for Barnsley College I played at right-back and ended up nearly starting World War III. It was at a time when I wasn't supposed to be playing because my grades were so bad, but Mark Ogley, our coach, picked me against an RAF XI. Mark may have regretted that decision when I went into a 50–50 challenge a bit too strong. I got the ball but also cleaned out one of the RAF lads, who wasn't happy about it, so it all kicked off. That was typical me – always trying to make up for my lack of size by getting stuck in.

Although I did have a bit of a growth spurt after leaving Wednesday – sod's law – there was still nothing of me. I looked young as well, so I couldn't really drink in pubs or buy booze before I was 18, because I'd always get asked for ID. But as soon as I was old enough I started going out for a few beers locally with a big group of lads. Collins, my old York County teammate and fishing partner, was one of them, and not long afterwards Jack Ridge and Josh Ranson, who are both a couple of years younger than me, came on the scene. Collins, who bears a resemblance to Verne Troyer, the actor who played Mini-Me in *Austin Powers*, works as a plumber. 'Rans' is nicknamed Frodo, after the character in *The Lord of the Rings*, and earns his living as an electrician. 'Ridgey' works in the care sector. They're all big Wednesday fans.

We'd usually get together at the Old Blue Ball, which is bang in the centre of Hillsborough. Everyone thought it was a dive as it had a bad reputation for a while, but I used to love it in there and never saw any trouble. It was a bit of a favourite with die-hard Wednesday supporters. They always had footie matches on the big screen, and there were dartboards, slot machines and a private pool table that the public weren't allowed to use because it was for league matches only.

I played pool for the pub on Monday nights. It was a proper league. You'd play at home and have to travel to different pubs for away games, much like football. You'd have a few pints –

Carling in the Ball because it was only £1.25 a pint – play your games and go home. I was still playing pool for them when I moved to Halifax in 2010, and I even got back to Sheffield for the odd game if they needed a player when I was at Fleetwood.

With reserve-team football at Stocksbridge not bringing any money in, I started working as a barman in the Malin Bridge Inn, which was only a few hundred yards from where we lived on Loxley Road. It had two bars and quite a big games room out the back, with a pool table, snooker table and a dartboard.

Some of the regulars would offer to buy you a pint while you were working, but you weren't allowed to drink while serving. You'd put it through the till to show that they'd paid for it, print the receipt off, circle the drink that was for you, put your initials on top and then pop it in the jar. When you went to the pub on a day off, you could ask for your receipts and have free drinks.

A lad called Danny Hirst also worked at the Malin. He was a few years older than me, and the two of us got on well (we still do – I'm godfather to his boy, Declan). One Saturday night, he asked me if I fancied a game the following morning for the Anvil, a local pub team he played for along with Crossy – the lad I used to kick a ball around with when I was younger – and Chris Szpajer, who were both regulars in the Malin. I hadn't met Chris before but, as with most people in our area, he was a big Wednesday fan, so we were sure to get on.

When you started playing regularly for the first team at Stocksbridge, you were put on a contract and couldn't play on a Sunday. But in 2006 I was still in the reserves, so I was free to do as I pleased. I wasn't going to turn down the chance to play another game. I'd have played seven days a week if I could.

The Anvil played in the Sheffield Imperial Sunday League, and Danny's dad, John, was the manager. Everything should have been straightforward in terms of signing and playing, even though it was so last-minute, but the match was in the cup and that presented a problem. At the time there were strict rules about registering to play for a team on the day of a cup tie, so we had to find a way around it. There was only one solution – I had to play under somebody else's name.

Glenn Maris produced his best performance of the season that Sunday morning. In fact, I'd go as far as to say that it was probably Glenn's best display of all time. I started on the bench – well, stood on the sideline, because they didn't have dugouts in the Imperial Sunday League – and came on in the second half, itching to get going. Within 30 seconds of being on the pitch I went on a run and hammered a shot that the keeper just about got his hands to and kept out. A few heads turned as if to say, 'What just happened there?' By the end of the match I'd scored twice and Les Jepson, the assistant manager, said to Danny as we were walking off the pitch,

'Where the fucking hell did you find him?' That was the first and last time I didn't make the starting lineup for the Anvil.

The story of my unofficial debut in pub football started to do the rounds. In Sheffield there was a Saturday sports paper called the *Green 'Un*, which carried reports from the previous weekend's games. The headline above our match report read 'Maris steals the show for Anvil'. I think Glenn would have been happy for me to carry on playing in his name every week.

I officially registered for the next match, and by the end of the season we were crowned league champions and I'd scored 50 goals, despite joining late. The standard was pretty shocking and we'd often be up against teams whose players were still drunk from the night before, in front of a crowd of about ten people – a few of them swigging beer cans on the sidelines.

We used to meet at the Anvil, on Stannington Road, and then fit everyone into the fewest number of cars possible for the 20-minute drive to Colley Park, in Parson Cross, where the matches kicked off at 11am. Whoever had not been out the night before was the designated driver, so that was never me. I'd usually been into Hillsborough or into town, and getting a good night's sleep to be at my best the next morning wasn't really a consideration.

The dressing room at Colley Park was a shed in the car park, so it was best to put your kit on in the car, and the pitch was usually covered in dog shit. There were no showers or toilets, so you were in trouble if you'd finished with a curry the night before.

As soon as the match kicked off I'd be having a bit of banter with the other team while I was running around – taking the piss and winding defenders up. I'd put it through someone's legs, call 'megs', and then put it back through them again a few seconds later. They'd try to kick me but I was too quick. I loved it. I felt like I could do whatever I wanted. There was no pressure, we were always winning and I was scoring every game. Danny still talks about one match when we found ourselves 4–1 down and, feeling pissed off, I said, 'Sod this,' ended up scoring four and we won 5–4.

After every game we'd go back to the Anvil. We'd still have our kit on, caked in mud, with everyone stinking. We used to have our own little corner in the pub, right next to the dartboard, so we were out the way of most of the regulars, who had come in for their Sunday lunch. We'd have a few beers, play a bit of darts, and then have sausages, roast potatoes and black pudding. I'd never tried black pudding before I played for the Anvil, but I soon found out what I'd been missing. It's still the best black pudding I've ever had – fried to perfection, not too dry, just right.

I think that's what I looked forward to the most. I loved football no matter what level I was playing at, but going back to the pub and having that lunch was brilliant. We didn't even have plates, just napkins, so you would pile it all up and put your food down at the table and your pint next to it. What more do you want? There I was with my mates, enjoying a Sunday roast and a beer in our football kit. I didn't have a care in the world.

Sometimes, after we were finished at the pub, I'd go home, get showered and then meet up with Danny. We'd go to the Malin for a couple of pints before heading off to the Yew Tree Inn. If we were in the mood, we'd go on to a club called Flares for a seventies night. Flares was open late and it was dirt cheap, not much more than £1 a pint, which was perfect for us.

Although it was Sunday morning football with the Anvil, there was a lot of local rivalry, in particular when it came to the cup final against Stannington Warriors. The match was played at Parkgate FC's ground, home to a decent semi-professional club in Rotherham, about a 45-minute drive from the Anvil. We took it so seriously that we got a coach to the ground and, for one game only, wore the Sheffield Wednesday strip, which their kitman, John Murray, who used to drink in the Anvil, let us borrow.

In the final I was wearing a pair of turquoise Adidas F50s, which made me stand out a bit and prompted one of their lads, just as I was about to take the kick-off with Crossy, to say, 'He'd better be good in those boots.'

I don't think I let him down. We won 7–2 and I scored four. But my favourite moment was when I sprinted off the pitch and back on again (a bit like Gareth Bale would in the 2014 Copa del Rey final, only this was the Imperial Sunday Cup final) to get around the full-back, a lad called Jon Wrigglesworth, and centre for Crossy to finish. Their centre-halves had a go at Wrigglesworth straight afterwards for not taking me out, shouting at him, 'Why didn't you fucking bust him?' He made the point that he did try.

• • •

Work-wise, I'd now moved on from being a barman and took a job as a trainee joiner. A bloke who drank in the Malin was manager of a construction company and asked me one day if I fancied working for him and I thought, why not?

I didn't really know what I wanted to do with my life then – it wasn't as if I had any aspirations or a career path. The only thing I'd ever thought about doing when I was at school was playing football, and my view on work was that as long as I had a few quid so I could afford to go out for a couple of drinks, I was happy.

It didn't take me long to realise that being a joiner wasn't what I wanted to do for the rest of my life. The days were long because the job we were working on was in Nottingham, so I was getting up at 5 in the morning to get there and do a full shift. By the time I got home I was so knackered that I'd go straight to sleep. It wasn't much of a life, and within four or five months I packed it in.

Danny mentioned that he could probably get a job for me at the Trulife factory where he worked in Sheffield with Crossy and Chris, and where his dad was production manager, so I thought I'd give it a go. I started on 1 February 2007, three weeks after my twentieth birthday, and went on to spend more than four-and-a-half years there. We had to clock in at 7:30am every day, Monday to Friday, which meant setting off at 7 every morning with Crossy. We'd clock out at 4:15pm – with a midday finish on a Friday.

The factory was open plan, so there was nowhere to hide, which meant that I kept getting caught texting when I should have been working. About 100 people worked there, so I took a little while to weigh the situation up. But once I'd got my feet under the table I started to be myself: loud and lairy.

Trulife manufactured medical products, and my job involved making carbon-fibre splints for disabled people suffering from drop-foot – a condition that makes it difficult to lift the front part of your toes and foot – to enable them to walk naturally. In that sense it was rewarding work, but it was also hard graft. Part of the process involved laying the carbon fibre onto a mould and then placing it in an oven to cook for two-and-a-half hours. They were heavy and awkward to slide onto the top shelf, which was almost as high as me, and I ended up with a lot of problems with my back.

The foot plate was about 12 inches, and the main part of the splint would go down the shin and then veer off to the side to go around the ankle. The splint could then be strapped to the leg with what looked like a shin pad. With the foot plate, you had to use a grinding wheel to get it to the size you wanted. You could wear whatever you wanted to work, but for that part of the job you had to put on a full bodysuit because bits would fly off, and if that stuff landed on your skin it was horrible – really itchy and actually quite dangerous. That's why you had to wear a mask and goggles as well, because if you were breathing it in, it was probably similar to asbestos. By the time you'd finished grinding, you were absolutely dripping with sweat.

I got the gist of it all and soon felt that I knew my line manager Mick Brown's job as well as my own, so if he wanted days off, he could trust me to handle things. It was up to Mick to finish off our work, right down to buffing the splint so that there were no sharp edges, and he would then bag everything up together, complete with a couple of Allen keys, so that the shin pad could be adjusted to suit the size of the leg. Then it was ready to be sent out.

I reckon the fact that I could stand in for Mick was the only reason I didn't get the sack for failing to turn up on so many Mondays – I took 36 off in one year alone and, not surprisingly, was nicknamed Sicknote. Danny was partly to blame for that, thanks to the hangovers I'd have after going out with him on a Sunday night.

Generally, though, I was happy working at Trulife. I was getting paid a full-time wage – a bit more than £1,000 a month after tax, more than enough to run a car and go out on a few evenings – and the job didn't conflict with my football, which was the most important thing.

We had a lot of laughs in the factory. Danny and I used to take pleasure in winding people up. We would pick up the biggest hammer we could find and, while someone was moulding, smash it down as hard as we could by the side of them. They'd shit themselves and jump a mile. On other occasions, I'd take a run at someone, often a poor guy called 'Cockney Jeff', slide tackle him to the ground and then everyone would pile on. Some people probably saw us as a pain in the arse, but all the messing around was just a bit of fun, harmless enough and helped to lighten the mood.

They were long, tiring days in the factory. Trulife had a lot of orders from hospitals, so we had to hit targets – about 400 foot-splints a week. It could be monotonous work, so building a bit of camaraderie helped to make the time pass quicker.

Occasionally, there was a chance to play a bit of football at work. We'd have a kick about in the car park during break-time, especially in the summer, when we didn't want to be stuck inside. We'd be pinging the ball to each other, trying to chip it into the rubbish skips out the back, often hitting people's cars in the process.

• • •

Not that long after I started at Trulife, I began to get a sniff of the first team at Stocksbridge. I got an early taste of how lively things could be at that level when I was on the bench at Cammell Laird, which is down on Birkenhead docks. We went to get on the coach after the game and saw that someone had put the windows through. It was a cold journey back to Sheffield.

A guy called Peter Rinkcavage was manager of Stocksbridge and, being honest, he wasn't for me. We just didn't get on. He never really gave me a chance, and I remember one away game in particular where we sat on the coach for hours to get there, only for me to warm the bench again. Rinkcavage brought me on with about 30 seconds to go, which didn't really improve matters.

But everything fell into place for me at the end of that season when Rinkcavage left to take over at Worksop Town and Gary Marrow replaced him as manager. Gary was an accountant by trade who worked for Rolls-Royce. He was in his mid-forties and knew the non-league circuit well. He'd been in charge at

Frickley, Belper and Grantham before coming to Stocksbridge, and I soon realised that he was my type of manager. He had a good sense of humour, wouldn't tolerate any egos and was big on team spirit.

Allen Bethel, the chairman, probably did Gary and me a favour early on by flagging my potential. Allen, who was in his early sixties when I joined, had watched me playing for the Under-18s and the reserves a lot, and he thought I had something to offer. A former credit manager in the local steel works, he didn't miss a trick when it came to Stocksbridge, because the football club was his life. Anything he doesn't know about Stocksbridge isn't worth knowing. He started the junior team in 1982 and was on the committee four years later when Stocksbridge Works FC merged with another club, Oxley Park, to form Stocksbridge Park Steels. Allen took over as chairman 12 months later and has been in that role ever since.

I think Allen was a bit disappointed that Rinkcavage didn't give me more of a crack at first-team level, and he probably worried that I might walk away if things didn't change. One day he pulled me aside and said that he'd told Gary that he thought I deserved an opportunity.

Gary was willing to give me a chance, but I didn't get off to a great start when I missed the first day of preseason. There wasn't much I could do about it, given that I was on holiday in Greece at the time. In any case, Gary soon realised that fitness wasn't going to be a problem with me. On my first day back in training, and only a few hours after getting off the plane, we did a 12-minute run and I absolutely smashed it. There was a central midfielder called Ian Richards, who was unbelievably fit and set the benchmark for everyone else. But I left Ian for dead in that session, and I think that helped me make my mark. Any running exercise like that was perfect for me, and it didn't make any difference whether I'd done any training or not in the lead up – and on that occasion I hadn't. I've always had pace to burn and endurance to go with it, as I proved on my military bleep test when I was at school, so preseason was never something that worried me like it does some players. I'm really lucky in that sense.

I knew that I also had to make an impact on the pitch to convince Gary I was worth playing. One of our early preseason friendlies was against Sheffield United and Gary was not around, so Mark Ogley, who had been appointed assistant manager that summer, took charge of the team. Mark must have remembered that game for Barnsley College against the RAF when I played at full-back, because he tried to start me there again until Gary spoke to him on the phone and said, 'Don't you dare!'

Centre-forward was where I wanted to play, but that wasn't always where I ended up. I used to be wide on the left a lot under Gary, which I didn't like. I didn't want to run back and defend – I just wanted to score goals. Defending is not exactly my forte, even though I'll work my balls off. I don't mind doing the ratting and pressing so that I can try to win the ball back higher up the pitch and put us straight on the attack, but tracking all the way back deep inside my own half, only for the ball to then be boomed aimlessly forward, isn't my idea of fun.

I was grateful, though, that Gary put me in the team, and he also claimed responsibility for my new nickname. We were playing away from home and the stadium announcer read my name out as 'Varney' rather than 'Vardy'. It made Gary laugh and reminded him of Reg Varney from *On the Buses*, so he called me Reg from that day on, and that's what the Stocksbridge lads still call me to this day.

Being in the first team meant that I was finally getting paid for playing – around £30 a week to be exact, and only during the season, from the start of August to the end of April. The majority of non-league clubs don't pay their players during the summer. The money was paid in cash and handed over in a little brown envelope, which sounds a bit dodgy but I can assure you that the tax was deducted at source. Allen will have the records to prove it, just like he's still got the handwritten transfer request I submitted on 26 January 2010.

When I was in Stocksbridge reserves there was never any danger of it clashing with work because we were playing in the Sheffield & Hallamshire County Senior League, so all the games were local, but it was different once I broke into the first team. We could be playing somewhere that was two or three hours away, and if that was a midweek game, which could easily happen towards the end of the season with our backlog of matches, I'd need to get off work early. Thankfully, I had a good boss at Trulife in John, and it also helped that we could take our leave in hours, rather than days, so there was never any issue when it came to getting to matches.

Training took place at Stocksbridge every Tuesday and Thursday night, unless we had a midweek game. I was nearly always the first one out on the pitch and I never wanted to come in at the end, which caused Allen a few difficulties because the floodlights had to go off at a certain time as part of an agreement with the local residents. At least that's what Allen claimed – Brett Lovell, the captain, thought it was more a case that the chairman wanted to save some money on the electric bill.

Once inside the dressing room it was always a race to get changed and in the shower because there was only so much hot water. I was always pissing about, getting up to all sorts, like grabbing the hosepipe, which was connected to the cold tap, and spraying everyone.

We had plenty of jokers in that team, but good players as well. Brett worked as a supplies manager for the NHS and in many ways he was Mr Stocksbridge. An experienced centre-half, he made about 300 appearances for the club over eight years and also ended up marrying the physio. Brett lived in Stocksbridge, so when we were playing at home I used to swing by his house and pick him up on my way to the ground, so that he could have a few pints in the bar after the game and then get dropped back afterwards. He said that he could hear me coming before he saw me because of the dance music blaring in my blue Renault Clio.

One of the biggest characters in our team was Ben Scott, our goalkeeper. In his full-time job he was a staff nurse, looking after patients, and in that role he obviously had to deal with some difficult situations, so I think that when he came to football in the evening, or on a Saturday, it was a form of release for him. At least that's my explanation for why he turned into a nutcase for two hours.

Ben had this thing about making animal noises. His impression of a horse was unbelievable. Sometimes, on the coach back from away games, he'd go through all the animals on request, even getting some of the supporters on board – who often travelled to matches with the players – involved too. What used to make me laugh most was when Ben would do it on the pitch in a game. The opposition striker would run clean through, one-on-one against him, and he would start barking like a dog or pretending to be a chicken to try to put them off.

Ben made the national news a few years after I left the club. He was sent off playing for Stocksbridge in a game at King's Lynn in 2013, and ended up saving a supporter's life. As he was walking off the pitch, he noticed a young girl running past him and asked her what was going on. She said that someone had died, so he followed her into the crowd and found a man, in his seventies, on the floor. Working with the St John Ambulance crew, Ben managed to get the man's heart back into a normal rhythm.

Non-league football is full of lads like Ben, larger-than-life characters who make the experience of playing semi-professionally even more enjoyable. It's a big commitment on top of your working week, probably another 15 to 20 hours when you take into account the travelling to training and matches, so the social side becomes almost as important as the football.

We'd all go to the bar after training, which Gary encouraged because it helped create that sense of togetherness. We'd also have beers on the back of the coach, bought by a supporter who travelled with us to the games and would go to Asda or Tesco beforehand and take advantage of whatever deal was on offer, bring the cans onto the bus and sell them off at a quid each until he got his money back. Anything he made on top of that he'd put back into the club.

• • •

One of the trips we looked forward to most was the end-of-season tour to Blackpool. There were no matches played – it was just solid drinking and a chance for everyone, including those who couldn't normally get a pass to go out on a Saturday night, to have a bit of fun at the end of a long, hard season.

We'd go up to Blackpool on the Friday morning, cram four of us in each car, get to the bed and breakfast where we were stopping, throw our bags in and head straight to the boozer. We'd all chuck a few quid in each and see how far it got us – usually about two bars. We'd drink all day, head back to the hotel to get changed for the evening and then go straight back out. We'd get three or four hours' sleep if we were lucky and then have another all-day session.

The manager and assistant always had single rooms. Everybody else shared, and we decided who went with who in our own version of an FA Cup draw on the back of the coach. Alvyn Riley, who was a quiet lad, got the short straw one year – he ended up sharing with me.

When we were out one night I bought a lightsaber – as you do in Blackpool. Alvyn had gone home early and taken the key to the room with him, so I couldn't get in later on when I got back. I was banging on the door, knocking hell out of it, and when he eventually opened up, I smacked him over the head with the lightsaber. I don't think he liked *Star Wars* much after that, and, to be fair, neither would I if I'd been on the receiving end.

On another occasion, three of the lads came back to the hotel dripping wet after they'd decided to jump into the sea at 5am. It probably seemed like a good idea at the time, but I don't thing any of us thought it was so clever when the landlady told us over breakfast that a guest had died recently after doing the same thing.

By the end of my first season at Stocksbridge I felt settled at the club. I'd made some good friends and I'd started to make a bit of a name for myself on the pitch. I think people could see that I had talent. I was quick, I could finish and I was never afraid to put my foot in, which non-league centre-halves probably didn't expect when they first looked at me and saw this skinny kid lining up against them. Yet getting another crack at the professional game wasn't part of my thinking in any way. I was just a working-class lad in Sheffield doing shifts in a factory, living at home with my parents and scoring a few goals for a non-league club that was a long way down the pyramid.

3

'SMASH HIM ON THE ANKLE, HE'S GOT A TAG ON!'

The handcuffs were tight, pinching into my wrists as I sat in the back of the police car, looking out of the window as the streets of Sheffield passed by in a blur. It was Friday morning, in the early hours, and I knew that I wasn't going to be sleeping in my own bed. I also knew that I wasn't going to be clocking on at 7:30am at Trulife and, strangely, that was troubling me more than anything else.

My hands were trapped behind my back but, with a bit of wriggling around, I just about managed to manoeuvre my mobile phone out of the pocket in my jeans without either of the policemen in the front of the car noticing. Chris Szpajer, my mate from work and the Anvil team, was handcuffed alongside me in the back, wondering what on earth I was trying to do.

I scrolled through my contacts until I got to my manager at Trulife. The text message didn't need to be long, not that it was going to be with a set of cuffs on. I punched in the keys on my Nokia, working from memory as much as anything, and pressed Send. 'Me and Chris Szpajer won't be in work today', the text read. I even managed to spell Chris's surname right – something the lads smiled about years later.

At the time there was nothing amusing. We were under arrest after a full-on two v two brawl outside a nightclub and on our way to West Bar police station in Sheffield, where a cell was almost certainly going to be our home for the night. West Bar is where Howard Webb, the 2010 World Cup final referee, used to work when he was a sergeant. It closed in 2011, and there's now a hotel on the site. I don't know what the new accommodation is like, but back then it was as basic as you would expect. Still, all things considered, I slept OK. A bit of alcohol in the system probably helped, as did the extra mattress and quilt that I asked for before I heard the cell door close behind me.

We were facing the possibility of being charged with affray at best and assault at worst. In the end, they had us for both. The first my mum knew of what happened was when I called her from the police station and asked her to get me a solicitor – I refused to do an interview without one. She wasn't happy with me, as you can imagine, but I wasn't one of those kids who never did anything wrong. I'd been in trouble before, and I was probably seen as the black sheep of the family because I was the first person to bring police to the front door. I didn't like to do anything that I was supposed to do – there was just something about living life on the edge that did it for me.

The incident never made the news at the time, unsurprisingly, but it has done plenty of times since. I wish the fight hadn't happened but I can't say that it keeps me awake at night in the same way as something that happened at a casino years later – I'd do anything to wipe away that horrendous evening. With the assault conviction, I've never regretted my actions. In fact, if I was put in the same position again, I'd do exactly the same thing, because I was defending a friend – someone I played football and worked with who had been mocked because of his disability.

Chris is five years older than me and was born deaf. His parents didn't find out that he couldn't hear until he was three years old. He had a really close relationship with his nan and would run into her arms whenever she walked into the room, but one day, when she came round to the house, he was sitting with his back to the door and didn't respond when she called his name. She did it again and again but there was still nothing, so Chris was taken for some tests. He was diagnosed as profoundly deaf, which means that he's always had to wear a hearing aid, from a toddler to the present day.

Although Chris lived locally, the first time I met him was when I was working in the Malin and he'd come in for a few pints. We got to know each other better when we played football for the Anvil on Sunday mornings before I started at Trulife. Soon we were going out in Sheffield for nights out, generally on a Thursday or Saturday, and the Leadmill was one of the places we'd sometimes end up.

A tall redbrick building close to the Hallam University campus in Sheffield city centre, the Leadmill is a music venue where some of the biggest names have appeared over the years, including Oasis, Coldplay and The Stone Roses. It was also a nightclub, popular with students as well as people like me and Chris, who didn't earn much and wanted cheap drinks.

We didn't set out with the intention of going to the Leadmill that night, and if we could turn back time we'd never have left the Malin, where we were having a few drinks and playing a bit of snooker after clocking off at the factory. But with the pints going down well, we decided to head into town to find somewhere a bit more lively.

We'd been in the Leadmill for an hour or two, having a laugh, throwing some shapes on the dance floor in between trying to chat up a few women – a standard night out for a couple of lads in their twenties – when some bloke got involved in an argument with Chris. It crossed a line when he started taking the piss out of Chris for having a hearing aid.

The two of them ended up head to head, the bouncers quickly got involved and, when they found out what was happening, they threw the lad out of the club and his mate followed him. That should have been the end of it.

I said to Chris that I thought we should just chill for a bit, let the dust settle and then go home. That's what we did, or at least that's what we planned to do. We left the nightclub about an hour or so later and started heading along Leadmill Road to get a taxi, when all of a sudden the two lads appeared. One of them squared up to Chris and started arguing with him, getting more and more angry. Then it all kicked off when the lad leaned in and, unbelievably, tried to bite Chris's nose off.

Chris had a bottle of Carlsberg he'd sneaked into his pocket to drink on the way home, as we often would in those days, and he used it in retaliation, hitting the lad over the head with it. His mate then tried to swing a punch at Chris when he wasn't looking, and that's when I got involved, doing what I think most people would in that situation – sticking up for a mate. It turned into a free-for-all, with everyone throwing punches.

One of the bouncers from the Leadmill came over, grabbed me and pushed me up against a car, before standing me up against the main doors to the nightclub. Chris and the other two lads were soon in the same position as we waited for the flashing blue lights.

After being charged we were released on bail, but the court proceedings rumbled on for ages. The floods in 2007 hit Sheffield badly during this time and pushed everything back. We appeared at a magistrates' court but the case was referred to Sheffield Crown Court because of the nature of the offences. By that stage I'd pleaded guilty. There was CCTV outside the Leadmill, so I didn't really have any option, even if I felt that I'd been left in an impossible position because of the way Chris was set upon.

When the case finally came around it was a relief in a way – we didn't want it hanging over us any longer. I turned up at court smartly dressed in a shirt and trousers and feeling a little apprehensive, but the prospect of going to jail really wasn't in my mind at first.

The mood shifted a bit in the waiting area, where you have a short meeting with the barrister before court starts. We found out that we had Judge Roger Keen QC. Keen had a reputation for sending people down when others might have taken a more lenient view, so we were told to prepare for the worst. Chris's dad gave him £30 to take to prison with him as he left the room – that was a measure of how serious things were starting to look.

In court it was a nightmare because Chris and I were in the dock with the two lads we'd been fighting with, literally sitting alongside one another. You can imagine how uncomfortable that felt. I can remember my barrister standing up and saying, 'I'm representing Jamie Vardy.' And when Judge Keen replied, 'Yes, we'll leave him to the end,' I was sure I was getting sent down. My mum thought the same. She walked out in tears and waited outside.

I glanced to my left, towards the entrance I'd walked in, and thought to myself, Shit, I won't be going out of those doors. There was another door behind me, where the security guard was standing, and that's the way down to the cells if you're off to prison, which is where I genuinely thought I'd be spending the next few months.

They played the CCTV footage in court and it didn't look good. Nor did the expression on the judge's face at the time. I maintained that I was only defending a friend, but the judge never saw it like that. He said I could have walked away, even though I told him that the two lads were waiting outside. If I'd left Chris to it I'd never have been able to live with myself, but I was wasting my time with that argument.

Judge Keen gave Chris and the other two lads their sentence – various amounts of time on the tag and community service – and then came to me. I stood up feeling sick with worry, the knot in my stomach growing tighter as I imagined what prison would be like – what it would mean for my life and my family.

Judge Keen said, 'You're lucky. The only reason I'm not sending you to prison is because I haven't sent any of the others.' I breathed a huge sigh of relief. Then he read out what he was giving me, which was a list that seemed to go on for ever. I ended up with six months on the tag, a 2-year supervision order with the probation officer, a fine, a 12-month suspended sentence, 280 hours community service, anger management – you name it, I got it. I stood there, listening to it all, thinking, *My life is done.* Forget playing football and going out for a drink with my mates – that had just vanished in front of my eyes. As I tried to take it all in, there was a split-second when it crossed my mind that it would have been easier to go to prison.

• • •

From that moment on my life was in lockdown. I had what looked like a rubber watch strapped to my ankle, which was horrific, and a home monitoring unit in the house. G4S came out to install everything, and we had to go through this exercise where I walked from one side of the house to the other on each floor so that they knew the boundaries of the property and could set the equipment up to send a signal to the monitoring unit whenever I was inside. I had a 6pm curfew and, make no mistake, that phone was ringing if I was a minute late.

At first the phone was installed in my bedroom, but it kept ringing every day at 1 and 2am, when I was trying to sleep, which drove me mad. I'd pick it up and they'd say, 'Who's this?' I'd say my name and they'd reply, 'It's showing that you're not in the house.'

It carried on like that for a while, so I phoned them up and, after spending ages trying to get through and report the problem, eventually one of the senior guys at G4S came out to look at the equipment. He was a decent bloke and clearly wasn't very happy with what had been going on. He thought that it was someone taking the piss at their end with the calls. After his visit I never had any issues with the phone ringing at odd times again. It probably helped that he moved the unit to the cellar, where I could no longer hear it even if it did go off in the small hours.

The tag and curfew didn't impact on my job at Trulife, other than in preventing me from doing any overtime. I think the top boss felt that I should have told him about it because he only found out when I explained that I couldn't work late one evening, but my manager knew what had happened from the outset and there was never any danger of me losing my job.

Initially, my football didn't suffer because the judge granted special dispensation for the first three months so that I could carry on training, as long as I was home immediately afterwards, and play in the away matches that would have made it impossible to be back by the curfew. The judge wouldn't let us give him the fixtures beyond the first three months because of the potential for games to be postponed and rearranged, so he asked us to send the dates of those matches closer to the time. Yet when that moment arrived and we applied for a similar arrangement it got knocked back, and I had no idea why.

All of a sudden I couldn't train or play in midweek matches, and we had to carefully pick which away fixtures on a Saturday were near enough to get me back home in time. If it was a two-hour drive I didn't even travel, and if it was less than that I'd play for about 60 minutes. Gary would substitute me early in the second half and my exit was planned with military precision. I'd get my kitbag ready at half-time and leave it in the dugout for one of the guys to give to my parents, who would then put it in the car to ensure that I could make a quick getaway. Then it was a race against time to get home.

For those who didn't know I was wearing the tag it must have looked a bit bloody odd to say the least. There was one game at Belper where I got subbed and just kept running, hurdling a fence around the side of the pitch and sprinting to the car, because Gary had left me on a bit longer than normal. It was like that American football scene in *Forrest Gump*. One of the opposition lads turned to Brett, our captain, and simply said, 'Where the fuck is he going?'

All the lads at Stocksbridge were fine about it and there wasn't any piss-taking – not that it would have bothered me if there had been. Once I told them what had happened and the circumstances behind it, there was no fuss. I got the feeling that any one of them would have done the same as me.

The opposition players never gave me any stick because nobody really knew I had the tag on – it just looked like part of my shin pad. There was one occasion when a lad who knew one of my mates was on the bench and he shouted out, 'Smash him on the ankle, he's got a tag on!'

He looked at me, I looked at him, and we both laughed and got on with the game. Wearing the tag on the pitch actually wasn't too bad in some respects, because I could adjust it so that it was protecting my ankle from any kicks I might get.

• • •

While football was stop-start with the tag on, especially after the first three months, my social life had ground to a complete halt. I was 20 when I was convicted, and my 21st birthday was just around the corner. I had to celebrate that landmark at home, which wasn't much fun, especially as all my mates were drinking out the front of the Yew Tree Inn that day – literally ten yards from my living room. Not wanting to miss out, I grabbed a bottle of Southern Comfort, held it up to them and poured myself a glass before tucking into the buffet that my parents had put on.

Confined to the four walls of my house for six months, I had a lot of time to kill after work, and much of it was spent watching films, helped by a bloke at work who sold four DVDs for a tenner. I racked up hundreds of movies, viewing three a night at one stage to try to escape the boredom. *American Pie* was a favourite, so I changed my Facebook status to 'lovin life, gettin paid, and gettin laid'. In truth, Finch, the character who came out with that line, was probably doing a lot better than me.

Not long after the tag went on I had to start attending anger-management classes once a week. I could only go on a Sunday because I was working full-time in the week at Trulife and playing for Stocksbridge on a Saturday. It was a ten-week course and it felt a bit like Alcoholics Anonymous – not that I've ever been. You had to get up in front of eight or nine others and say your name and what you were there for: 'My name is Jamie Vardy and I assaulted someone,' that kind of thing. I was in a group with people from all walks of life, including some who had just been released from prison and others in need of a fix.

One week there was a guy by the side of me who was shaking. He kept saying to me, 'You all right, mate?' Over and over again he was doing that and it was really getting to me. So when it got to the lunch break I said to the tutor, 'You need to move him. He can't sit by me. He's going cold turkey. Just look at him.' Miraculously, he came back after the break and was fine. He'd obviously shot up. Anyway, I did the full course and at the end of it I got a certificate to say I'd passed. Quite what that meant I don't know, but it ticked a box for someone.

As the weeks and months went by I kept going back to the probation officer, telling them what they wanted to hear: that I wasn't going to reoffend and that it was a one-off. And to be fair to the probation officer, as soon as I explained what had happened and why it happened, they kind of understood why I'd ended up in that situation.

Once I finished the anger management classes I started to get through the community-service hours. You'd turn up every Sunday and there would be a list of different activities going on, things like painting, gardening and cooking. There was a supervisor on each activity and they were only allowed to take so many, so if they already had the full quota you had to go and do something else – something you probably didn't want to do. In my case that was decorating. Repainting the walls and skirting boards in a school wasn't a job that I ever thought about taking up in the future.

For a few weeks I found myself working at a community centre where the grounds surrounding it were like a dump. We'd go in every Sunday and try to turn it into a proper garden area, planting things and generally tidying it up. Thankfully, I could wear whatever I wanted while doing these activities – none of that high-vis jacket nonsense. Stick one of those on and people take one look at you and think, You're a criminal, I'm not having you doing this.

Another time, I did some cooking for pensioners. I'd go to a sports hall, where they'd all come for their Sunday dinner, and then help the chef prepare and cook the food. I'd serve it, do the washing up and then leave everyone in the hall playing bingo. That was one of the occasions on community service when I could see that I was helping people and doing something genuinely useful.

Obviously, you never want to put yourself in a position where you end up having to do jobs because of a criminal offence, and I certainly didn't like giving up my Sundays, but some good did come from it now and again. I also met one of my best mates there.

• • •

Grant Willhouse would go on to become the final member of the Inbetweeners – a name that Becky, my wife, gave to the four lads I class as my closest friends. I first crossed paths with Grant at a community-service woodwork centre. I think I was making a chessboard with blue-and-white squares – for Sheffield Wednesday, obviously. There was never much chance of it being mass-produced in the club shop at Hillsborough, though, or of Grant buying it – he's a Sheffield United fan.

The other three making up the Inbetweeners are Collins, Rans and Ridgey, my drinking pals from the Old Blue Ball. They're all from Sheffield and they've known me since I was a nobody. They come to as many matches as they can – people I've played with at all levels have enjoyed their company – and you generally know when they're in the room.

When G4S came out to take the tag off I was finally able to get back to spending time with the Inbetweeners and the rest of my mates. Relieved to have my freedom back, I went to Blackpool for the traditional end-of-season tour with Stocksbridge and had another run-in with the police, only this time they saw the funny side. It was a Saturday morning, so we were just about to get back on the beers after a big session the previous day, and I went into a joke shop on the promenade and bought a scary old man mask. I put it on and the first people I decided to scare were two coppers. I jumped out in front of them as soon as I got out of the shop. Fortunately, they had a sense of humour, but I don't think Gary Marrow could believe what he was seeing.

A little while after that came a more worrying brush with the law at the Malin Bridge Inn. To this day, I couldn't tell you what led to the incident or who was responsible for it because it just happened totally out of the blue. All hell let loose and I was lucky not to lose an eye.

There was a party on at the time, so there were wooden boards over the top of the snooker and pool tables to prevent the cloth getting ripped or damaged. Unfortunately, my face didn't have any protection. One minute I was talking to Danny Hirst, my pal from the factory and the Anvil team, and the next thing I knew I'd been glassed. I rushed to the toilets and looked in the mirror to see my face covered in claret. By the time I came out it was like a scene from the Wild West – people scrapping left, right and centre.

Danny's missus and her nan were there with him, and even the nan was getting stuck in. Everywhere you looked, people were fighting – I'd never seen anything like it in the Malin. It wasn't long before I was taken outside and put in the back of a police car. I hadn't even done anything but I looked a right state.

I was calm while I was talking to the police officer, who was actually pretty sound. 'Are you all right? What happened?' he asked.

'No, I'm pissed off,' I said. 'Look, it doesn't matter what's happened, but I'll tell you what's going to happen. Your sergeant is going to go into that pub, look around, come back out and charge me with affray.'

The copper said, 'Nah, he won't – you'll be fine. I can see you've been glassed.'

When the sergeant came out, he gestured for the police officer to go over and speak with him. To be fair to him, he walked back over to me afterwards and said, 'Well, you were right.'

I said that I needed to get my face sorted out at the hospital first, so I got put in the back of the police car with no handcuffs on. After a little while they pulled up on the side of the road, shone a torch in my face and decided that I didn't need to go to hospital after all, so they took me straight to the police station. As soon as we got there, the sergeant on the desk took one look at me and asked the officers why they hadn't taken me to get some medical care. So we got back in the car and went to the hospital, where we obviously should have gone in the first place.

The nurse had a look at my eye and said I was extremely lucky that the glass had just missed it. I ended up having the area around it glued, and then I was taken to a police station in Ecclesfield, not far from where the Anvil used to play at Colley Park. Eventually, they decided that they weren't going to bring any charges, so I was free to go home.

● ● ●

Looking back at that period of my life, I think I lost my way a little and didn't really know what to do with myself. At the time it felt like everything was OK, that I was earning a few bob, playing football and getting up to all sorts with my mates – just having a laugh, really, without worrying too much about what was to come. But I can now see that I was a bit wild and didn't really have any focus or direction.

Everything had been channelled into trying to make it as a professional footballer for so long, and there was no contingency plan. I hadn't prepared for failure in life – in fact, I don't like to plan for very much at all. So there was nothing to fill that huge void that Wednesday's decision to ditch me had created. I was lost, I guess – and I didn't even realise it.

At one stage I even tried to sign up for the Army. In my head I was thinking about not just the military aspect, but having the chance to play sport while I was in there. I knew that Guy Whittingham had gone down that path before carving out a career as a professional footballer, playing for Sheffield Wednesday in the process, so it seemed worth exploring.

I went to the recruitment office in Sheffield town centre, started filling out the application form and saw the section asking about criminal records. Obviously, I had to tell them the truth – it would come up anyway in a background check – so I just circled 'Yes'. I told them what had happened and they said there and then that I couldn't apply. It seems strange now to think that I could have ended up on the frontline. Maybe the discipline of the Army would have been good for someone like me.

I'd got into a few scuffles when I was younger, in particular in the period after I was released from Wednesday, when my dreams had been shot, my head was all over the place and I'd decided that education wasn't for me. I think I was in that period of life when you're just not sure where you're going or who you are.

Even going to watch Wednesday wasn't incident free. I started to go to a few away games when I wasn't playing on a Saturday – even though I was devastated that they'd let me go, Wednesday were still my team. Going to an away game on the train meant the police would escort you en masse to a pub prior to going to the stadium, so that there was less chance of any trouble.

There was a similar arrangement in place after the match, with the police shepherding you to the station. At Derby station after a game at Pride Park, however, we ran into problems with the police, who were stopping people getting on the train. I wasn't looking to cause any aggro, but a copper blocked my way and said, 'You're not getting on.'

'Yeah, I am,' I said.

That same conversation went back and forth a couple of times, until I went to walk past him and he stuck his nut on me, helmet and all. I still had a deep mark across my forehead to show for it by the time I got home.

The way I saw things back in those days was that trouble came looking for me rather than the other way around. There always seemed to be someone who fancied having a swipe – at least that's how it felt when I was growing up. Admittedly, I probably didn't help myself sometimes. I could be a bit mouthy and I'd always stand my ground in a confrontation, but that's just me. I'm not the sort of person to take a step back. And that doesn't mean I can't handle myself. It's more a case of thinking, What's the worst that can happen? You get sparked out.

Or, to borrow another phrase, chat shit, get banged.

4

'YOU'LL PLAY
FOR ENGLAND'

'This is the year for you, Jamie. We need to get·you in the
League. You've got everything. It's all there for you. If you
perform like you did against Mossley, you can do whatever
you want in this game. You can go on and play for England.
That's how good you are.'

Before John Morris finished talking I burst into laughter.
We were in the sitting room at home in Malin Bridge. My
mum, who was standing in the doorway listening, turned
on her heel and walked into the kitchen shaking her head. It
was the summer of 2011 and I was playing for FC Halifax
Town in the Blue Square Bet North, two tiers below the
Football League, still working in a factory in Sheffield,
and I had a football agent in front of me saying that I

was going to play for my country one day. 'You can't be serious,' I said.

But he did mean it – every word of it. He'd just watched me score two and set up another two in a preseason friendly against Mossley on their sloping pitch at Seel Park. It was a scorching July afternoon, the surface was bone dry and the grass a bit long but I'd run riot, carrying on where I'd left off the previous season. The fact that it was against a side a couple of leagues below Halifax didn't seem to matter to John one bit. 'I love your pace and aggression. You play with a real edge to your game,' he said.

John was working for a company called Key Sports, who looked after Theo Walcott and a number of other Premier League stars, as well as Championship players and some lower-end professionals. They didn't have non-league footballers on their books and, not surprisingly, John wasn't being encouraged to recruit any. There's not much money to be made in the sixth tier of English football, and very few players rise from that level to the top.

I found out that John had come across me following a tip-off from Phil Senior, who was the Halifax goalkeeper and had been in Huddersfield's academy when John coached there, long before he became a football agent. 'You need to come and have a look at this player,' Phil told John. 'He's a lunatic, but he's single-handedly winning us the league.'

John watched Halifax several times without me knowing, then got hold of me on the mobile – that took a while because I'm always dubious about answering phone numbers I don't recognise – and arranged a face-to-face meeting. He was in his early thirties and turned up at my house suited and booted, with not a hair out of place. I hadn't gone to the same effort and answered the door wearing a pair of shorts, wondering why this bloke was wasting his time with me. John's employers were probably thinking the same.

He hadn't been working for Key Sports long, but had done a few deals in Greece and managed to shift Charles Itandje, Liverpool's out-of-favour goalkeeper. Now he wanted to pick up some clients of his own. John sounded ambitious and talked a good game – beyond that, I wasn't sure what to think. Players in the Blue Square Bet North didn't have agents.

In the end it was a bit of a no-brainer to sign up with him, especially when he explained the financial terms. Agents normally get a percentage of your wages as part of the agreement to represent you, but John said that he wouldn't take a penny off me until he got me into the League. So I saw it as a win-win situation and, deep down, didn't imagine that it would ever cost me anything. I couldn't see there being much chance of me turning professional at the age of 24.

John, however, was a lot more optimistic. He handed over some glossy brochures with pictures of Walcott on the front, and the next thing I knew a financial advisor was knocking on my door and talking to me about career-ending insurance and banking. That was a brief conversation because I was lucky if I had anything in my account. I also had a PA called Sarah, who could get me concert tickets at the drop of a hat. More usefully in my case, she would take a phone call at 11 o'clock at night to put me on a guest list when I was struggling to get into a nightclub in Sheffield. It felt like I was being treated like a Premier League player, yet I was earning £350 a week, driving a knackered Saab and getting ready for the opening game of the season against Corby Town.

According to John, that situation wouldn't last much longer. He told me about some of the contacts he had in professional football and promised that he would get people along to watch me play. That side of things hadn't really been a problem in the past, though. During my last two seasons at Stocksbridge plenty of scouts turned up, and the same was true after I signed for Halifax in the summer of 2010. The bigger issue was convincing those managers, coaches and scouts to take a punt on me.

Crewe Alexandra were sniffing around for a while, and in January 2009 I went there on trial for a week. Crewe were a League One club at the time, and I took part in a practice match on a 3G pitch, which wasn't ideal because I don't think you can ever show your true ability on that sort of surface. It plays so differently to grass and I can't get up to full speed on artificial turf – and pace is obviously a big part of my game.

Gary Marrow, the Stocksbridge manager, came down to watch me in a match played at Crewe's training ground and he thought I did OK. They played me out wide, as Stocksbridge often did, rather than as a striker, and Crewe clearly weren't convinced by what they'd seen. Gudjon Thordarson, the former Iceland coach, was Crewe's manager back then, and afterwards I was told that he wanted someone with more experience. 'He's certainly not going to come in and help us this season', was the quote that Neil Baker, Crewe's assistant manager, gave to the local paper. That suited me fine, because I couldn't wait to get back to Stocksbridge.

I realised early in my trial that signing for Crewe didn't interest me one bit. I'd always played with my mates, and all of a sudden I was around people I didn't know, which felt strange and uncomfortable. I had to use a week's leave at the factory to go there and, as far as I was concerned, I got nothing out of the experience whatsoever. There were two young lads staying in digs with me at the same time, so I asked what we did for dinner. They said they'd been to the supermarket and were making some pasta. I didn't fancy anything like that, so I went round the corner and found a McDonald's. I wasn't going to try to be something I'm not.

Later that season I had a trial with Rotherham United, who were in League Two and managed by Mark Robins, the former Manchester United striker. Rotherham phoned Stocksbridge afterwards to say that they wanted to sign me on a short-term deal until the end of the season. They offered about £2,000, which the club weren't very happy with but felt obliged to tell me about. 'No chance,' was my response when I heard Rotherham's proposal. I wasn't going to give up a full-time job and play for Rotherham for a few months only for them to potentially say at the end of it, 'Thanks, but no thanks.'

Sheffield United were also in the mix and one of their scouts seemed to have a Stocksbridge season ticket. He obviously saw enough in me to keep coming back – but not enough to persuade him to get the club to make an offer. Maybe watching me get sent off a few times didn't help. I got four red cards in a little over twelve months, including three in my final season at Stocksbridge.

Then again, that Sheffield United scout was wasting his time in the first place. It wouldn't have made any difference if he'd thought I was the next Lionel Messi or Cristiano Ronaldo, because there was no chance I was ever going to sign for Sheffield United. No matter how much money they offered me, no matter what league they were in, no matter how big the opportunity, I'd never play for Sheffield United. I'm Wednesday through and through – always have been, always will be. It's in my blood, blue and white.

Plenty of other professional clubs were rumoured to be interested in me, but I couldn't say how genuine their interest was and, to be honest, I was never in a hurry to find out. I know that Allen Bethel, the Stocksbridge chairman, said after I left that I couldn't have had a great deal of ambition when I was playing for them because not only did I spend so long there – the best part of seven years – I also seemed perfectly happy to do so. And he's probably right. The ambition was there when I was at Wednesday but it drained away the moment they let me go. You soon stop dreaming of being the next David Hirst when you're working in a factory and approaching your mid-twenties.

Also, those seven years at Stocksbridge gave me a lot of enjoyment, so it wasn't as if I was in a rush to leave. I certainly didn't play for the money – £120 a week was the most I ever got paid at Stocksbridge. I did it because I loved football and I was around people that I liked. I looked forward to training and playing for them because of the spirit among the lads – and the fact that we also had a bloody good side.

In 2009 we won promotion to the Unibond Premier Division – three tiers below the Football League – for the first time in the club's history. I was one of four players who scored

20-plus goals that season – Mark Ward, Andy Ring and Carl Fothergill were the others. Wardy had been a professional at Sheffield United, and in terms of technique he was probably the best player at the club. He was a window cleaner by trade and Brett Lovell, our captain, worked alongside him for a while. Carl was also up and down a ladder because he was a firefighter. Ringy, by virtue of his ginger hair, was called Ralph Malph from *Happy Days*, and he went on to make more than 300 appearances for Stocksbridge.

A personal highlight for me that season was fulfilling a lifetime ambition by running out at Hillsborough. This time there was no security guard trying to chase me off the pitch as we beat Brodsworth Welfare 3–0 in the Sheffield & Hallamshire Senior Cup final. The photos of us celebrating afterwards went up on the wall in the boardroom at Bracken Moor. Standing alongside my teammates, I'm bare-chested, with a massive grin on my face, a bottle of champagne in my hand and a Stocksbridge flag draped around my shoulders. A picture of happiness if ever there was one.

To win promotion we had to beat Belper in a one-off play-off tie at their ground, and nobody wanted to leave anything to chance because it was such a big opportunity for the club. Brett was so concerned that I might go on the piss the night before the match that he got me to stay at his house in Stocksbridge, where I slept on the sofa.

One incident in particular was probably playing on Brett's mind. On New Year's Eve that season I danced on the tables in the Malin Bridge Inn and staggered home in the early hours, on the same day that we were playing Goole away. I can't even say that I'd got a bit carried away, because it wasn't one of those nights when you plan to have a quiet one and it somehow turns into a session. When I left the house that night it was my sole intention to see in 2009 drunk.

I woke up feeling absolutely horrendous. But, after looking out the window and seeing everything frozen outside, I thought that it was only a matter of time before the game was called off. Sure enough, plenty of fixtures did end up falling victim to the weather that day, but, unbelievably, our trip to Goole, in East Yorkshire, wasn't one of them. So I had to get myself together as best I could.

I turned up late for the game, which was unlike me. Although I'd ring in sick for work at the factory if I had a bad hangover, I always reported for football – and in good time. I tried to blag it by saying that I couldn't find the ground, but Gary was no fool. He knew exactly what had gone on from the moment I set foot in the dressing room, and so did everyone else. I was seeing double and not really with it at all – I even looked pissed – so I got changed and tried to keep my head down, sneaking in and out of the toilet to avoid eye contact with Gary.

Outside it was bitterly cold, and Victoria Pleasure Grounds, Goole's stadium, wasn't living up to its name or doing much to inspire me. There's a running track around the pitch, two giant water towers dominate the skyline and trains rumble by. I wanted to jump on one of them and get home.

I don't know what anyone was expecting from me that day, but by half-time I got the impression that there wasn't going to be much of an inquest into what I'd been up to the previous night. I'd scored twice and we were on our way to a 3–0 win. My second, a left-foot shot from 25 yards that arrowed into the top corner, was a beauty. Brett looked across at Darren Schofield, our left-back, and just started laughing. I've no idea what Gary made of it, but he could hardly give me a bollocking.

• • •

In those days I didn't worry too much about what I was drinking or eating. Fast food was part of my staple diet, and I'd often go to Burger King or KFC for my pre-match meal when we had a midweek game. In some ways it was a case of needs must – I was in a rush leaving work and just needed to get some food inside me a few hours before kick-off.

I'm lucky in that whatever I did off the field never seemed to affect my performance. I was always full of running, loaded with aggression and prepared to go toe-to-toe with a defender, no matter how big the player I was up against. Gary used to wince sometimes when he saw me go in for a challenge. Whether it was a 50-50 or 90-10 against me, I'd never pull out. Sometimes I got the ball and on other occasions, like against Ashton United in March 2010, I got the man and a straight red card. The blessing on that occasion was that it was right in front of the steps up to the dressing rooms at Bracken Moor, so I didn't have far to walk.

I ended up missing 20 games in my final season at Stocksbridge through a combination of injury and suspension, and I still scored 19 goals. People said that my disciplinary record probably discouraged League clubs from taking a chance on me, which may well have been the case. But I always felt that I needed to play with that fire inside me, partly because of my size. I wasn't the biggest, and almost everyone I came up against was a big lump, a centre-half who wanted to kick the shit out of me. I wasn't going to just stand there and take it.

At times it became a little game to see how much you could get away with off the ball, because when you're playing at that level there are no cameras and only three people who can catch you. You learn to take it and give it out. Sometimes the red mist came down and it was in full view of the referee, like it did when I came up against a lad from Kendal Town in September 2009. I don't think either of us liked the challenge we'd both gone in for, so it all kicked off and I gave him a jab. The two of us were sent off.

That was my first match back from suspension, and the chairman was starting to get pissed off because he was paying me while I was banned. I saw his point of view, but at the same time I wasn't going to change how I played. The good, I like to think, outweighed the bad, with the solo goal I scored at Gigg Lane that season against FC United an example of what I was capable of. I put the afterburners on to run with the ball from inside our half and glide past a couple of their players before steering a low shot into the bottom corner with my left foot. FC United filmed the goal, complete with commentary – it's on YouTube – and there were 1,888 there to see it, which was the biggest crowd I'd ever played in front of at the time.

Unfortunately, Gary had resigned as manager a couple of weeks prior to that match after falling out with the chairman. It was a big disappointment for quite a few of the lads, including me, and the team started to break up, which prompted me to submit a transfer request in January. I was under contract at the time, so the only way I could get out of Stocksbridge was if someone paid money for me. Luckily Halifax did, but I had to wait four months, and by that point there was someone else in my life.

• • •

Ella Vardy was born on 25 April 2010. I met Emma Daggett, Ella's mother, a few years earlier. We'd see each other a couple of times in the week, but she'd go out with her friends on a weekend and I'd go out with mine. It wasn't really a close relationship, so when Emma fell pregnant in the summer of 2009 neither of us really knew if we were ready to be parents.

We decided that we wanted to keep the baby, but about four months down the line we agreed that we shouldn't be together just because Emma was pregnant. It could have messed Ella's life up even more if we had tried to make something work for the wrong reasons.

I made sure I was there when Ella was born because I wanted to be and, as the father, it was only right. There wasn't time to get emotional when Ella arrived because she wasn't breathing at first. I could barely get my head around what was happening as the nurses took her straight away, and I felt useless standing there like a spare part – but then came her little cry. We were so relieved to hear it.

Later that day I took Emma and Ella back to Emma's parents'. It wasn't an easy situation at the time, and it hasn't been over the years. I asked Emma what she wanted for Ella – I wasn't going to get up and leave and not provide. I wanted to pay my way and I also wanted to be in Ella's life. But I didn't see much of Ella in the first six or seven months. Then, suddenly, I heard from the Child Support Agency.

Ella's arrival gave me extra motivation on the pitch. It wasn't all about me any more, and I needed to make some extra money, too. The move to Halifax in May 2010 offered me the chance, but it also showed that I needed to work on my negotiation skills. While maths has always been a strong point thanks to Mr Pemberton's round-the-clock times tables, I certainly didn't have Halifax backed into a corner with my wage demands.

John wasn't on the scene at the time, so in the absence of an agent I travelled to Halifax with Gary Marrow, who had returned to Stocksbridge as manager after patching up his differences with the chairman. We had a chat on the way about what I should ask for, bearing in mind that Halifax had agreed to pay £15,000 for me, which may sound like peanuts but it was a lot of money for that level of non-league football. Gary and I agreed that he'd leave me to it once it came to getting down to the nitty gritty with David Bosomworth, the Halifax chairman.

I thought I'd push the boat out and go for £250 a week, a bit more than double what I was on at Stocksbridge. The chairman said that was fine straight away, and I was so pleased I almost snapped the pen out of his hand. In hindsight, I probably could have asked for more.

Halifax had just won promotion to join Stocksbridge in what had been renamed the Evo-Stik Premier Division. Yet it didn't feel like a sideways move, and that's no disrespect to Stocksbridge. Halifax were a former Football League club that had gone bust and set their sights on getting back up the ladder as quickly as possible. The set-up was still in place from the League days, and they'd been averaging gates of close to 1,500 at The Shay compared to the couple of hundred who watched at Bracken Moor.

Neil Aspin, who made hundreds of appearances for Leeds United and Port Vale across the 1980s and 1990s, was Halifax's manager. Neil had been a tough, imposing defender back in his playing days, but he had a calm air about him as a manager and we got on fine. When I first met him, Neil told me that he'd been following me for a long time, going back to when he was in charge at Harrogate, another semi-professional club. It turned out that he'd tried to watch me quite a few times at Stocksbridge one season and wondered why I was nowhere to be seen at some midweek games. I was at home with a tag around my ankle, of course.

After I joined Halifax, Neil got calls from other managers saying that they wouldn't have signed me because they'd heard I could be a bit lively. But I never once let him down on that front. I think Neil actually liked the fact that I had a bit of devil in me.

It was a big ask for him to convince Halifax to pay £15,000 for me, but I think any doubts about the size of that fee and whether it was seen as a risk were put to bed after a game I played for Stocksbridge up at Durham City in February 2010. David Bosomworth was one of 87 people to turn up on a cold

Tuesday night in the North East to see us win 5–1. I scored two and set up another, and by the end of the evening he was on the phone to Neil, joking with him at first that he had wasted his time travelling up there, before telling him that he'd do all he could to sign me.

After spending so long at Stocksbridge, it seemed strange to be going to another club for the first day of preseason. Stranger still was that we were going to be on a running track. It wasn't something we'd ever done at Stocksbridge, so I didn't have the right footwear. I had no option but to use the sort of trainers you'd wear more casually with a pair of jeans. Not that it made much difference – I pissed it, and quickly felt at home.

As Sheffield to Halifax was a bit of a commute – about 40 minutes longer than the journey to Stocksbridge – I got together with a few other lads to share the driving and save a few quid on petrol, which is the sort of thing that happens all the time in non-league football, otherwise you'd end up playing almost for free. I'd travel with Danny Holland, another striker, Lee Gregory, a forward who joined on loan from Mansfield, and Jonathan Hedge, a goalkeeper. When it was my turn to drive, everyone piled into my Saab and, put it this way, we were never late.

Neil had assembled a strong team at Halifax, and it soon became clear that we were too good for the league we were

Chasing the dream with Sheffield Wednesday Under-15s. That's me grinning on the front row second from the right. I had no idea that heartbreak was around the corner and that the club I supported would soon let me go. The lad kneeling on the far left is Danny Care, who went on to play rugby union for England.

Still just a lad, here's me playing for the Under-18 team at Stocksbridge in the 2004/2005 season where I finished top scorer.

© CHRIS SZPAJER

The Anvil pub team that won the Sunday Imperial Cup. Those turquoise Adidas F50 boots I was wearing caused a bit of a stir before kick-off. Three of the lads I worked with at the factory played in the same side. Danny Hirst is stood behind me slightly to the left, Ashley Cross is immediately behind him to the right, and Chris Szpajer is alongside the keeper.

© PETER REVITT

Aged 21 and already mastering the art of the goal celebration, although not too many were in the crowd to see me score the winner for Stocksbridge Park Steels against Kidsgrove in April 2008.

Celebrating winning the Sheffield and Hallamshire Senior Cup with my Stocksbridge Park Steels teammates in April 2009. It was a special occasion for me because the game was played at Hillsborough – at least that's my excuse for getting on the champagne.

In action for FC Halifax Town, who I joined from Stocksbridge for £15,000 in the summer of 2010. I handled all the contract negotiations myself and picked up £250 a week for my efforts. We won promotion as champions from the Evo-Stik Premier Division in my first season with the club.

Celebrating a goal with Danny Holland against Corby Town in August 2011. Danny and myself became a bit of a double act at Halifax with our post-match interviews.

Looking fresh-faced not long after joining Fleetwood Town for £150,000 at the end of August 2011. I quit my job at the factory only a few days before signing and never looked back.

© CHRIS BULL / ALAMY STOCK PHOTO

Look closely and you'll see an Oompa Loompa, Batman and some Crayola Crayons in the crowd. My mates from Sheffield decided to introduce themselves to Fleetwood on an October afternoon in 2011 as we beat Bath City 4–1. I scored twice and the bar takings went through the roof.

© DERICK THOMAS

Celebrating my first goal for Fleetwood Town in 2011. We won 3–2 against Kettering and a lot of the lads said that day was the moment they realised why the chairman had been willing to pay all that money for me.

A third promotion in four seasons for me, this time as Blue Square Bet Premier champions with Fleetwood, to take the club into the Football League for the first time in their history. I finished the season with 31 league goals.

The smile on my face says it all. In May 2012, at the age of 25, I finally fulfilled my ambition of becoming a professional footballer when I signed for Leicester City. Fleetwood received £1m for me – a record fee for a non-league player.

Lloyd Dyer and Anthony Knockaert celebrate my equaliser in a 2–1 win over Middlesbrough at the Riverside Stadium in September 2012. It was my fourth goal for Leicester since joining from Fleetwood. I scored only one more that season as I badly lost my way, even contemplating quitting.

Another bottle of champagne, another promotion – this time with Leicester in April 2014. Everything came good for me in my second season at the club as I scored 16 goals and we won the Championship title to reach the Premier League.

Leonardo Ulloa embraces me after setting up his first goal against Manchester United in September 2014 in a game I'll never forget. I scored on my first Premier League start and had a hand in the other four goals in an incredible 5–3 victory over Louis van Gaal's team.

© PA IMAGES

© PA IMAGES

A fist pump from Claudio Ranieri after I got the winner against Crystal Palace in October 2015. I quickly hit it off with him after he took over as manager that summer, but he didn't always want to be tuned into my frequency!

A magical moment as I run away to celebrate after beating Manchester United's David de Gea in November 2015 to break Ruud van Nistelrooy's record and become the first player to score in 11 successive Premier League matches.

© PA IMAGES

© PA IMAGES

My opening goal against Liverpool in February 2016 and I doubt I'll ever score a better one. I saw Simon Mignolet, the Liverpool keeper, off his line as I ran onto Riyad Mahrez's pass and from well outside the area thumped a bouncing ball over his head.

A red card followed by the red mist. I let Jonathan Moss know exactly what I thought of his decision to give me a second yellow card for diving against West Ham in April 2016. It was my first sending off as a professional footballer and the finger-jabbing earned me an additional one-match suspension.

© PA IMAGES

in. We were winning almost every week, and my own form started to take off at the turn of the year, when I scored seventeen goals across three months, including one against Stocksbridge that left me looking miserable. Quite a few of the players I'd lined up alongside the year before were still playing for the club, and it just didn't feel right to celebrate. I thought a lot of those lads – I still went to Blackpool on tour with them after joining Halifax – so I wasn't going to rub their noses in it. Instead, I walked back to the halfway line with my head down.

I hadn't been able to play in the away game at Stocksbridge earlier in the season because of a foot injury, but I'd gone along anyway to watch. One of the things that struck me straight away was the brand new dugouts sitting on a strip of newly laid concrete in front of the main stand. When I bumped into Allen Bethel, the Stocksbridge chairman, he said, 'We used the money we got for you to get all this sorted out.' I wasn't sure how I felt about being worth the same as a couple of benches and a few bags of cement, but maybe there was a compliment in there somewhere.

It didn't take Halifax long to realise that they could be looking at a bigger return on their investment. The chairman was talking about me in glowing terms, ridiculously so, in my eyes. At one point he claimed that I was better than Andrei Arshavin, the Russia international playing for Arsenal at the time, and he also said that the second goal I scored against North Ferriby, when I turned those afterburners on again, was one that 'Lionel Messi would have been pleased with'. Personally, I was happier with the last-minute winner I scored against Chasetown in March to complete my hat-trick. If you watch the goal on YouTube, you can see one of our lads stop for a moment and put his hands on his head, almost in a state of shock at what he's just seen.

Halifax had their own in-house media team, which had continued from their Football League days and would have been almost unheard of anywhere else at that level, with the possible exception of FC United. The idea of giving filmed interviews post-match was something that was totally new to me and, to be honest, seemed like a great chance to lark around and just be myself. Danny Holland was usually my partner in crime, and he was standing alongside me after that Chasetown match as I was asked to talk through the goals. I got to the last one and, with a deadpan expression, said, 'Well, the third speaks for itself.'

Life was fun. The Inbetweeners and a few of the other lads from Sheffield would often get a minibus over to watch me play and I wasn't taking anything too seriously. Maybe that helped on the pitch because I just kept scoring. Four days after the hat-trick against Chasetown, I got another three against Kendal Town and marked the last goal with a new celebration.

I bent over, pulled down my shorts and revealed a pair of red Playboy slips that had 'Lucky Pants' written across them along with a couple of dice. I was on a roll and just missed out on a hat-trick of hat-tricks in the space of eight days when I got two against Nantwich Town.

Sadly, something happened during this period that put everything into perspective. Trevor Storton, our assistant manager, died on 23 March, aged 61, after a long battle with cancer. We were all devastated when we heard the news. I got the match ball from the Chasetown game signed by all the lads and gave it to the manager to pass on to Trevor's family. We never suffered another defeat that season – perhaps fittingly, given the loss of Trevor – and won automatic promotion as champions.

• • •

Scouts kept coming to The Shay, especially after that flurry of goals in March, but nothing ever went any further. Doncaster Rovers asked to take me on trial, which I think Neil saw as a bit of a cheek given that they probably wouldn't have entertained the idea of a bigger club asking to borrow their best player for a while. Neil even recommended me to several League clubs, including a few in the Championship, but they didn't want to know.

Halifax were aware that they were onto a good thing, because a few weeks before that 2010–11 season came to an end they offered me an improved three-year contract, which saw my pay go up to £350 a week. I put pen to paper but cast doubt on my future a few weeks later in another tongue-in-cheek interview with the Halifax media team. Asked on camera if I could clarify whether I'd stay with the club, I replied, 'No, I'm signing for Ibiza Town. I'm going to Ibiza on holiday and I'm never coming back!'

By this point the Jamie Vardy and Danny Holland double act was in full swing, and at our end-of-season awards dinner they asked the two of us to do a piece to camera, almost Ant and Dec style – except those two obviously know what they're doing. 'Keep on rolling,' was the request from the cameraman after we ran out of things to say, so I started doing forward rolls, in my best gear, across the floor at the Cedar Court Hotel in Bradford. I believe the footage appeared on an end-of-season DVD.

It was around this time that John Morris came on the scene, and it quickly became clear that Halifax weren't impressed that I had an agent. John turned up for a meeting with the chairman and David Bosomworth just looked at his watch and said, 'You've got five minutes.'

That set the tone for some difficult exchanges I didn't get involved in. John needed to establish how much Halifax wanted for me, and £150,000 wasn't the answer he was looking for. He felt it was ridiculous to ask that much for someone who'd not even played at the highest non-league level, but the chairman wasn't budging.

Undeterred, John got a number of managers to come and watch me. Paul Peschisolido, who was in charge of League Two side Burton Albion, saw me play twice and I scored in both games. Peschisolido described me as 'quick, lively, tenacious and aggressive', but wasn't comfortable with paying that sort of fee for someone playing at such a low level.

A few days after the Mossley preseason match, John persuaded Lee Clark, who was manager of League One side Huddersfield Town, and Terry McDermott, his assistant, to see me in action in a friendly back at my old club Stocksbridge. I set one up and scored two in a 4–1 victory, but when Clark spoke to John the next day, he said he wasn't prepared to go beyond £30,000 for me. Halifax were never going to entertain that sort of offer. It felt like I was trapped and, in fairness, I probably hadn't helped the situation by extending my contract before John got involved.

John made the point to Halifax that they were standing in my way, denying me the chance to get into the Football League and turn professional. I could see things from the club's point of view – they'd won another promotion and didn't want to lose me – but I was 24, not a kid, and the clock was ticking. John kept pushing, fighting my corner and talking about me in a way that made me think he believed in me far more than I believed in myself.

There was a bit of a standoff with Halifax, so I decided to take what was a huge gamble at the time. I walked into Trulife and told John Hirst, my boss, that I was leaving. I'd been there for four-and-a-half years and I felt that my body, especially my back, was in bits because of the physical nature of the job, so I thought I'd quit, have a year living purely on my football wages and see where it could take me. I was kissing goodbye to about £20,000 a year and all the security that came with it, but that was a sacrifice I was willing to make to get some respite from work.

John, my agent, never knew anything about my decision until I rang him up and told him what I'd done. He sounded a little surprised and maybe felt a bit more pressure to find me a club, given that I was going to be training on Tuesday and Thursday evenings and playing on a Saturday with nothing else in between. But it wasn't my intention to turn up the heat on him, because I knew that he was doing everything he could.

With no sign of any club willing to meet Halifax's demands, and with me working my notice period in the factory – thankfully in the warehouse so I wasn't lifting the moulds into the oven any more – I lined up against Corby on the opening day of the season totally in the dark as to what the future held for me.

5

THE ADOPTED SCOUSER

'What do you know about Fleetwood Town?' John said.

'Nothing,' I replied. 'Never heard of them.'

'Go and google them and find out as much as you can,' he said.

'Why?' I asked.

'Because you're signing for them tonight.'

By the time we walked into the De Vere Whites hotel across the road from Bolton Wanderers' ground later that evening, I'd established that Fleetwood was near Blackpool and they played in the Blue Square Bet Premier, one level above Halifax and one below the Football League, but that was about it. Andy Pilley, their ambitious chairman, soon filled in the gaps. The club had won four promotions since he took over as chairman, and he had no intention of stopping there.

A new £4.5 million main stand had not long been finished and Andy, who funded everything out of his own pocket, was on a mission to get Fleetwood into the Football League. He didn't want it to happen sometime in the future – he wanted to do it that season.

In an ideal world, I would have been sitting across the table from a Football League club, but nobody would pay Halifax the £150,000 they wanted. Fleetwood had tried to negotiate on that valuation and get me for £75,000 plus add-ons, but were given short shrift. Yet, unlike other clubs, Fleetwood weren't put off. When they did agree to hand over the full sum, David Bosomworth, the Halifax chairman, told John that he had never felt so sad to receive so much money.

The way I saw it, Fleetwood was not only a step into the unknown, but also a shop window. They were a non-league club run on a professional basis, so for the first time in my life I was going to be a proper footballer, training every day, not just a couple of evenings a week. Everything about it felt good, right down to the idea of running around with my name on the back of my shirt. 'Vardy' up in writing – I liked the sound of that.

I scored my last goal for Halifax in a 1–1 draw with Colwyn Bay on the Tuesday – the same day I finished at the factory – and later that week, on Friday 26 August 2011, I became a Fleetwood player. Now I was going to be playing football for a living and earning more money than I could ever have imagined. John agreed a three-year contract with Fleetwood worth £850 a week, which was an absolute fortune to me.

I even made the national news. Well, five short sentences appeared on the BBC website – 75 words in total – under the headline 'Fleetwood Town sign FC Halifax midfielder Jamie Vardy'. They got my position wrong, but that was easily forgivable – even my new teammates had never heard of me. A number of them had played in the Football League and found it strange that Fleetwood were spending so much money on a player from a lower level. Andy Mangan, or Mangs as we called him, a centre-forward I ended up getting on brilliantly with on and off the pitch, admitted to me later that, when he first heard about my arrival, he thought, Who on earth are we signing for £150,000 from Halifax?

It probably was a bit of a gamble on Fleetwood's part, but it was one that the chairman was willing – and able – to take. Andy Pilley was a self-made millionaire who set up his own utilities business in 2002, around the time he got involved with his hometown team Fleetwood. Within a decade, Business Energy Solutions were turning over £40 million a year and Fleetwood had been transformed. By the time I signed, Fleetwood was a Football League club in everything but name. Highbury Stadium had been totally redeveloped and you could feel the level of expectation around the place, not least because it filtered down from the man at the top.

I think the chairman saw me as the missing link in his plan to win promotion, and he was determined to get the deal through in time so that I could make my debut on the Friday night – within 24 hours of our meeting – at home against York City. Micky Mellon, Fleetwood's manager, was also present at the hotel meeting, and I got the feeling from him that I'd be on the bench against York and would come on at some point. So when I got to the ground on the evening and Micky called me into his office to say that I was going straight into the team, I was a little surprised. In the dressing room, Steve McNulty, the club captain, must have thought that he needed to put me at ease, because he came up to me and said, 'Don't worry, just play your normal game.'

I just looked at him and said, 'I'm not worried.'

Steve and I would laugh about that conversation later in the season, and he'd tell me that he thought I was a 'lairy little bastard' at the time. I was just being myself – not being fazed by anything, least of all football. Once I'm over that white line I'm in a zone, thinking about football and nothing else. And football means enjoyment to me, not pressure or worry or stress. I didn't manage to score on my debut, but I was named man of the match and left the ground with three staples in my head after one of the York centre-halves sunk his teeth into me in an accidental collision.

We were playing Wrexham away next, on the Bank Holiday Monday, and although the other lads went in for a cool-down after the York game, Micky let me have a couple of days off to move everything up from Sheffield. When I got on the coach to go to Wrexham, the lads started having some banter with me straight away, saying, 'Didn't fancy coming in for the cool-down, then?'

I just laughed it off, but then Jamie McGuire, one of many Liverpudlians in the squad and another Fleetwood player who would go on to become a good mate, asked a question in front of everyone that stopped me in my tracks: 'Vards, why were you on the tag, lad?' I just looked at him, lost for words for once in my life, thinking, How the hell do you know about that? I had no choice but to tell the story.

We ended up losing 2–0 at Wrexham, who were top at the time, leaving us eight points behind them only six games into the season. The pressure was on to start putting some victories together, and we got up and running at Kettering the following week, when I scored twice in a 3–2 win. A lot of the lads talk about that game as the moment when they realised why the chairman had been willing to pay all that money for me. I think it wasn't just my goals but my pace that surprised people. I gave one of the Kettering players a ten-yard start before scoring my second.

• • •

I soon started to feel as though I was in a good place at Fleetwood. Training every day – which I was doing for the first time in my life at the age of 24 – was making a difference, and it also helped that I wasn't knackered from a five-day week at the factory before I'd even kicked a ball. I'd always had my speed, but now I felt sharp and fresh as well. I was playing five-a-side games when I once made carbon-fibre splints, and working on my finishing instead of trying to dink the ball into one of the skips in the car park at Trulife.

I also had my independence for the first time. As Fleetwood was nearly a two-hour drive from Sheffield, there was no way I could commute, so I had to leave home – something I couldn't afford to do before. Fleetwood made everything easy for me. I was given a relocation allowance and the chairman owned a former bed and breakfast in Lytham St Annes, a really nice area not far from Blackpool, where I lived with a few of the other lads when I first signed.

I soon moved into a four-bed detached house in Thornton – another property that belonged to the chairman – along with Rob Atkinson, who was a centre-half, Peter Till, a good-looking lad who loved himself, and Junior Brown, an absolute legend who had a massive afro and was addicted to getting tattoos. It was a nice house that, after a few months of us living there, benefited from the employment of a cleaner. The chairman likened the state of it to a scene from *The Young Ones*.

Although so much had changed in my life in such a short time, everything about Fleetwood felt right, especially the lads I was playing alongside. The easiest way to describe our dressing room would be to say that it was full of nutters – a lot of them Liverpool lads. I managed to fit in with their sense of humour straight away, and it wasn't long before they were calling me an adopted scouser. Steve McNulty also nicknamed me 'the Cannon' – I think the word 'loose' belonged in there somewhere – because I was always up to something, setting a few grenades off and leaving others to pick up the pieces.

On one away trip I sneaked into chief executive Steve Curwood's hotel room and turned it upside down. A little while afterwards, Steve discovered the scene, came downstairs, looked at me – guessing I was involved straight away – and said, 'Didn't do a very good job, did you?' So I gave it a few minutes, went to reception, got another key card, and with the help of Jamie McGuire absolutely ransacked his room and sprayed shaving foam everywhere.

I was probably able to get away with antics like that because I was doing the business on the pitch. I took my game to another level that season, helped by full-time training, the quality of the players in our team and the confidence I gained from seeing what I could do in a better league. I seemed to be scoring almost every week, and they were goals of every description, which left the chairman saying that it felt like it was cheating having me on the pitch.

I never saw it that way. We were a team full of good players. Jamie Milligan, who was at Everton as a kid, had a tremendous left foot. He played for England Under-18s in a midfield that included Steven Gerrard, Scott Parker and Joe Cole, and he had Premier League appearances to his name. We nicknamed him 'the Island' because he had a receding hairline with a lone tuft of hair at the front, which he refused to shave off. Mangs, who was a terrific character and never short of a word, scored 20-plus goals. Gareth Seddon, a part-time model who'd retired from the professional game through injury, weighed in with his share and so did Magno Vieira, who claimed he was born in Brazil but in the eyes of all the Fleetwood lads was really from Wigan. I could namecheck all the players, really, because everybody in that team was capable of playing in the Football League.

The gaffer was the one who pulled everything together. Fleetwood was Micky's first job in management. By the time I arrived he'd already been in charge for three years, and he was still only in his late thirties. His approach was to go all out attack, sometimes with four forwards on the pitch, while off the field he encouraged us to have a good laugh and often joined in with the jokes. But he also knew where to draw the line, and if we let him down in a match – which happened later in the season – we knew about it.

Micky played me everywhere: out wide, through the middle and in the hole. He used to say that I had the ability to turn anger into energy, because he felt that everything was 'dead aggressive' with me but, by and large, controlled. I was guilty sometimes of making challenges that were probably borderline red cards, but Micky never tried to curb that streak in me, because he knew what I knew: without that I wouldn't be the same player. I would put everything on the line every game, not just for me, but for the team.

I strayed the wrong side of the law only once that season, when I got sent off against Kidderminster for a two-footed tackle that threatened to do more damage to one of my own teammates than any of the opposition. The ball was running loose, one of their lads was coming towards me, with both of us sprinting full pelt, so I thought I needed to go in hard, otherwise I was going to get hurt. And that's what I did. I missed the ball, missed the player and nearly got Mangs instead. A three-match ban followed.

While suspended, I went along to watch us play at Stockport, and Peter Crouch was in the crowd. He was sitting on some tiny old-school wooden seats with his knees up around his ears. Crouch was dating Abbey Clancy, whose brother Sean played for us. Sean was also in a TV programme called *Desperate Scousewives*, which was every bit as bad as the title suggests. One day, they turned up at Fleetwood's ground to film, and the chairman thought it would be good for publicity for the club to get involved. I remember walking out to the car park with Mangs and getting a phone call saying that they wanted all the Fleetwood lads to be in an episode. We looked at each other and thought exactly the same thing: Fuck that.

We were quite happy to stay under the radar. I was fairly active on social media – tweeting now and again and occasionally updating my Facebook status – but I was a non-league footballer and nobody particularly cared what I did or said. If I got a few comments back I was lucky.

There was no shortage of entertainment at the training ground, where something always seemed to be going on. We had some boxing gloves in the gym for use on the punch bag, but Jamie McGuire put them on one day and got in the middle of a makeshift ring with Richard Brodie, one of our strikers. The majority of the lads stood around the outside while three of us – Steve McNulty, me and Nathan Pond, who was the club's longest-serving player – were the judges. Everything was done properly, right down to a couple of the other boys acting as trainers and offering a few words of wisdom when the bell went at the end of each one-minute round. The winner got to keep the belt and then had to defend it against someone else.

We trained at Fylde Rugby Club in Lytham St Annes, which is on the Irish sea and bitterly cold for six months of the year. The wind would really cut through you, so the last thing you needed was to get naked. That was among the punishments handed out if you arrived late or trained badly, and one day I found myself doing a lap of the pitch with nothing but my boots on. Thankfully, the only people watching were the lads on the balcony pissing themselves laughing.

• • •

Not long after signing for Fleetwood, I developed a new routine to help put a spring in my step: three cans of Monster energy drink a day. I'd have one can as soon as I got up to get myself going, and another two before training. When I got to the training ground, it was sometimes a case of, Shall I go to the gym? Nah, let's have a can of Monster.

Jamie McGuire was doing the same, and a few people started to get concerned about how much we were drinking because of the amount of caffeine in each can. One day in training my body just packed in – I had absolutely nothing in me and I felt horrendous. We both got pulled in by the doctor and advised to cut back, which we did. We went on to Red Bull instead.

I was still going out on the town drinking, the only difference being that I wouldn't do it the night before a match because the standard of football was a lot better than I'd experienced before. I knew I couldn't get away with it. When I did venture out, my usual rules applied: only go home when the club shuts. Sometimes, if we had a day off on a Wednesday, I'd go back to Sheffield for an R&B night called Chocolate Tuesdays, stay over and drive back first thing on Thursday morning. I'd leave extra early to avoid the traffic, taking Snake Pass through the Peak District to get to the training ground in good time. I'd then set the alarm on my phone, put the seat back and get my head down for an hour in the Saab before anyone arrived.

I ran into a rich vein of form over October and November, when I scored nine goals in eight games, including five in as many days against Alfreton Town and Bath City. The Bath game was memorable not so much for my two goals, but for the costumes in the stands. About 20 of my mates from Sheffield, including a couple of the Inbetweeners, introduced themselves to Fleetwood that day. They quickly made their presence felt to everyone – from the players to the chairman and the supporters, and especially the bar staff, whose match-day takings must have gone through the roof.

They'd all come in fancy dress. Rans was an Oompa Loompa, Ridgey was Batman, four of them were Crayola crayons, and Superman also made an appearance. One of the lads was dressed as a woman and, if I remember rightly, he was putting his leg up onto the bar that you lean on when you're standing on the terraces and lifting his skirt.

I scored in the first half, but it was in time added on, so the 'Barmy Army' were nowhere to be seen as they'd already gone inside to get a drink. My other goal arrived late in the second half, this time in front of them, but as I'd already been booked I didn't go all the way over to them to celebrate in case I got sent off. Rans wasn't as worried about any punishment that might come his way and was dancing on the pitch in his Oompa Loompa outfit. Later on, we all went out in Blackpool – my mates and the Fleetwood lads – for a typically low-key evening.

We won the next league game 2–1 at Kenilworth Road, where I put us ahead with a left-foot dink over the keeper, but nobody was talking about the goals on the way home. Richard Brodie caused a major fracas that afternoon. He had some history with Luton, and he was winding them up so much that their players went for him at half-time. There was a massive stand-off in the tunnel as we all lined up and made a barricade between Brodie and the Luton players. Once we got into our dressing room, the police came in and said to Brodie that if he carried on and ended up causing a riot, they'd lock him up. Thankfully, we all got out in one piece and with the three points.

* * *

Scouts were now watching me in numbers and I was making myself the centre of attention in more ways than one. When the other lads grew moustaches for Movember, I decided to be different and have a mohawk. I had my hair shaved to grade 1 on the sides and let it grow long on top for several months so that I looked like a punk rocker. With the help of Danny Moore, the kit man, I even dyed it red for one game. John, my agent, wasn't too chuffed about it because he didn't think it created a great impression on the scouts who were coming along to see me play.

I let my boots do the talking in the FA Cup, where we knocked out two League One clubs, Wycombe and Yeovil Town, to reach the third round for the first time in Fleetwood's history. I scored in both ties, and we all knew the significance of winning at Yeovil in a replay because the draw had already been made. We were playing Blackpool, our Championship neighbours. With the two clubs only nine miles apart, it was a huge match for us and in particular for Andy, our chairman, who grew up supporting Blackpool.

'Genuinely, hand on heart, we would prefer Blackpool at home to Manchester United, Manchester City, Tottenham, Liverpool – anybody,' he said. 'The hysteria this tie will cause for the next few weeks will be absolutely immense.'

The transfer window opened a week before we played Blackpool, and there was a lot of speculation about my future.

My agent told me that Leicester and Southampton were showing serious interest, while Cardiff and Peterborough had made inquiries. It was also reported that West Ham United, West Bromwich Albion, Sunderland, Fulham and Wolves were considering making bids. It felt a bit surreal to hear those clubs mentioned, but I just kept my head down and focused on Fleetwood and the Blackpool tie.

Our preparation for the match was far from perfect because we were burgled the night before, while we were all sleeping. I was the first one up, and when I went downstairs I could see that the TV was gone. Peter Till used to take it up to his room sometimes when everyone had gone to bed, especially if his girlfriend was staying over, so I knocked on his door. When he said that he didn't have it I woke up the other lads as well and said, 'I think we've been robbed.'

We had a mini snooker table in the conservatory, where we found my cue unscrewed. The burglars must have walked round the house with the butt-end in case any of us woke up. All of which meant that we spent the morning of the Blackpool game speaking to the police and their forensic experts.

I wouldn't go as far as to say we were also robbed in the match, but the 5–1 scoreline flattered Blackpool big time. It certainly wasn't a true reflection of the game because we played some really good football. I got our goal and also generated a few headlines for giving Alex Baptiste, who would later become a good friend, the run-around. Ian Holloway, Blackpool's manager, described me as a 'wonderful player' afterwards and said that he'd 'never seen anyone run as beautifully'.

About ten days later Micky took us away to his native Scotland for a mini-break, and I decided to have a bit of fun and send the rumour mill into overdrive. There was speculation in the papers that Celtic and Rangers wanted to sign me – I didn't know whether it was true or not – and after we touched down I tweeted: 'Just landed in Glasgow'. The next thing I knew, it went crazy. My phone was bombarded with messages, and I got my first taste of dealing with the national media when a load of journalists were waiting for me after we played Motherwell in a friendly.

While nothing came of the Celtic and Rangers stories, Holloway's praise was genuine and led to Blackpool making a bid for me straight after the FA Cup tie. Andy Pilley, the chairman, called me one day after I'd left training and asked me to go to his office at the ground. He told me that they'd had an offer from Blackpool but it was nowhere near what they wanted for me. He basically said that if someone came in with a £1 million offer he would let me go, and that was my agent's understanding of the situation too.

I went back to concentrating on my football, and I didn't think any more of it until we played away at Forest Green Rovers on 28 January 2012, when deadline day was approaching. We'd left training to meet the team coach at the Windmill Inn when John told me that two clubs, Leicester and Southampton, had offered Fleetwood £1 million for me. That was the trigger for a deal to happen as far as I was concerned, so I didn't see any point in getting on the coach.

Micky hadn't got to the Windmill Inn at that point, but word had got back to him that I was refusing to travel to Forest Green, so he called me. He explained that any transfer business was nothing to do with him as the manager, and he ended up talking me into getting on board. He spoke to me again when we arrived at the team hotel, told me to forget about it all, to get my mind on the game and that it would be sorted out afterwards.

But for the first time in my life I didn't want to play a football match. I'd just turned 25 and, finally, after all those years playing non-league football, trying to bounce back from my disappointment at Sheffield Wednesday, I was going to get a shot at the big time. What if I played at Forest Green and got a serious injury?

By the time Saturday morning came, nothing was any clearer. John spoke to Andy and told him that I wasn't in the right frame of mind to play. He made it clear that he didn't think it was right to block such an incredible opportunity for me. I didn't even have time to digest how amazing it was that clubs were willing to make me the first ever £1 million non-league player. All I could think about was the possibility of signing for a big club.

'You're not going anywhere,' Andy finally told me. 'I've not spent £150,000 just for five months. We spent that money to get promoted, and all those lads that you train with every day, they need you as well. You're letting them down if you walk out now. I want Fleetwood to be in the Football League next season and you're the main reason that's going to happen. Now go and finish the job.'

I felt that Andy had gone back on what had been agreed, and he'd put the £1 million price tag on because he thought nobody would come up with that sort of money for a non-league player. My agent wanted me to be in the Football League as soon as possible, and I felt the same way. I'd quit my job to concentrate on football, and one of the thoughts turning over in my mind was whether the same clubs were going to come back in for me when the season was over.

In the end, I had no choice but to accept that I was staying. Once the transfer window closed there was nothing I could do. I spoke to the lads about it, said how pissed off I was, and I even went as far as refusing to celebrate when I got the equaliser against Tamworth the following Saturday.

But while I was angry and frustrated, I wasn't going to throw my toys out of the pram and allow it to affect how I played – that's not my style. I'm not selfish. I'll always play for the team, and that showed over the next couple of months when I scored 11 goals in as many matches after the Forest Green game.

During that run I registered my second hat-trick of the season in a 6–2 win over Ebbsfleet. I scored the first with my left foot, the second with the outside of my right and the third from just inside the centre circle, when I spotted their keeper off his line and lobbed him.

A lot of what I did back then was off the cuff. Some lads who've been with professional clubs their whole lives only know one way to play, because that structured approach has been drilled into them constantly. They've been in an academy playing development-squad games against another bunch of kids who've been brought through exactly the same way.

Other than when I trained with Wednesday, I'd never really had someone saying, 'This is what you've got to do.' I certainly didn't have that during my seven years at Stocksbridge, where nothing was too regimented and I had the chance to express myself. I can remember how the manager, Gary Marrow, would often do a little exercise in training where we had a 50-yard pitch with a goal at either end. He'd kick the ball into the middle and you'd just play one-on-one. I loved it. It was like those kickabouts in Malin Bridge, where I felt that I could do whatever I wanted.

At Fleetwood I had that same sense of freedom, which was credit to Micky, who gave everyone the opportunity to thrive with his tactics. In early March we made it 10 wins out of 11 away at Kidderminster, on an evening when Roy Hodgson, the West Brom manager, came to watch me. The surface was awful and I didn't have one of my best games. In fact, my agent thought I was a bit lucky not to get sent off for a lunge near the touchline.

Five goals followed in my next four games, and I had a new nickname, courtesy of Peter Cavanagh, another Merseyside lad. When we beat Mansfield 2–0 at home in March 2012, the front page of the *Non-League Paper* showed all the boys pointing to the sky after I'd scored our second. The reason for that celebration – and I know this sounds ridiculous – is that they'd started to call me 'God', supposedly because of the ability I had to produce goals from nowhere.

Not that our team needed any divine intervention. Come early April we were unbeaten in 27 league games across six months and on the verge of creating history. We faced Wrexham, who were in second place, at home on a Tuesday night, knowing that victory would seal the title and clinch promotion in a league where only the champions are guaranteed to go up. But in front of a crowd of just under 5,000, Wrexham held us to a 1–1 draw and we then squandered another chance to wrap things up three days later, when I scored my 30th and 31st league goals of the season to help salvage a point against Lincoln.

Crossy, my mate from Trulife, came across to watch that game, along with a few of the other Sheffield lads. I asked the chairman for an executive box for them, and they couldn't have been happier when they won £900 on the club raffle too. The plan was to go out afterwards, on the back of winning promotion, and then go to the Grand National at Aintree with the Fleetwood players the next day, as we had the Saturday off.

But back in the dressing room, Micky was fuming. 'You think I don't know where you lot are going tomorrow?' he said. 'Fucking think again. I'm not bothered about tomorrow, but if any of you go out tonight after that result, I'll have you.' I thought, *Shit. Do I or don't I?* In the end I did the sensible thing and stayed in while my mates went out.

I certainly made up for it on the Saturday. It was an all-dayer at Aintree, and the beers tasted even better when we found out that we'd won promotion to League Two. Wrexham could only draw at home with Grimsby, and Blue Square's Alan Alger gave us the good news, as well as £150 worth of free bets each. In the *Non-League Paper* the next day there was a picture of all the lads holding 'Champions' flags at Aintree. Well, all the lads apart from me.

I'd gone to the bar to get some beers in, and when I returned to where I'd left my teammates, nobody was there any more. I stood there holding all the drinks for a while, thinking, Where the fucking hell is everyone?

It turned out that they'd gone off to have that photograph taken, leaving me looking like a waiter who couldn't remember which table he was serving. Everybody eventually returned, and I reluctantly did a radio interview with Steve McNulty. I say 'reluctantly' because I was already pissed.

We all went out together in Liverpool afterwards to cele-brate. I was stopping at Jamie McGuire's mum and dad's house, together with Rob Atkinson, but we ended up losing each other at some point and I had to get Mangs home because he was in a bit of a state. I got the taxi to stop at McDonald's before pulling up at Jamie's parents' house. The lads still weren't back and I didn't want to wake up Jamie's mum and dad, so my only option was to get in the Saab. I worked my way through 20 chicken nuggets and then sat back and went to sleep, only to be woken by laughter and a tap on the window a little while later when the lads eventually got home.

• • •

We decided to have some fun in the final match of the season, against Luton. A few months earlier we'd given 'the 50p game' a try, and with nothing riding on the Luton result we thought it was time to revisit it. The rules are simple: someone walks out onto the pitch with a 50 pence piece in their hand, which has to be passed among teammates while the game is going on. You can't give it back to the player who has just given it to you, and whoever ends up with the 50p at the full-time whistle has to get a round of drinks in after the match.

It's obviously all supposed to go on discreetly, but against Luton we got caught by the referee, who took the coin off us and handed it over on the sideline – a bit like a teacher might confiscate something in a classroom. When we got a throw-in by the dugout, Danny, our kit man, gave the 50p to the player taking it and we carried the game on. At one point Mangs went down injured when I had the coin, so I saw it as a perfect opportunity to hand it over. I think Scotty Davies, the goalkeeper, ended up with the 50p at the end. And that was Fleetwood in a nutshell: brilliant but mental.

Work hard and play hard was the motto in our squad, and that suited me perfectly. It was the third time I'd won promotion in four seasons, and by now I had a good idea of what was needed to build a winning team. Ability's important, but that alone will only take you so far. You need spirit and togetherness as well, and at Fleetwood we had all of that and more.

I think everyone at Fleetwood knew that Luton was going to be my last game for the club. Andy had promised to let me go at the end of the season and, to be fair, he didn't mess me about. He could have turned it into an auction and tried to drive up the transfer fee, but he never went down that path. I think he respected the fact that I didn't sulk and just got on with the job he asked me to complete. In the end it worked out exactly how we all wanted it to – Fleetwood won promotion to the Football League and I got my big move. So I don't feel anything bad towards Andy. He's sound, and anyone who's passed through Fleetwood knows what he's done for that football club.

One of my final acts as a Fleetwood player was to attend the end-of-season awards, where I pretty much swept the board without ever properly getting my hands on the trophies. They were so big that I left them there when we went out for a few drinks afterwards, assuming they'd find their way back to me. Jamie McGuire took them home and said he'd pass them on, but they've never surfaced and I doubt they ever will – they're probably sitting on his mantelpiece now with his name engraved on them.

Not long after I left I thought I'd call Micky to see if he fancied catching up for a drink – I wanted to say thanks to him for everything he'd done for me. We met in a pub called the Fairfield Arms and, as well as pulling out a bottle of champagne, Micky made me promise him that I'd go back to Fleetwood when I had a 'fancy car' and pump the horn outside the Portakabin that was his manager's office. And that's exactly what I did once the old Saab was traded in for a Range Rover.

6

SKITTLE VODKA

As I got changed at Belvoir Drive, pulled on my boots, made my way out of the dressing room and set off on the short walk up to the practice pitches at Leicester City's training ground, I decided enough was enough. I couldn't stomach it any longer and I was going to deal with it the only way I know how – head on. I saw Nigel Pearson, the Leicester manager, and made a beeline for him before the session started. There was no point beating around the bush – I just needed to get it off my chest. 'Gaffer, I want to go back to Fleetwood on loan,' I said.

I wasn't doing it for a reaction. I meant it. The move to Leicester wasn't working out for anybody and I didn't see any value in going through the motions for the final few months of the season. I was in a downward spiral, where I was drinking too much – some of it home-brewed – and not scoring nearly enough. My head had gone, and at one stage I had even talked about giving up football and going to work in Ibiza. It was a throwaway comment that probably confirmed what the management team already knew: things weren't going well for their summer signing.

I knew that I could return to Fleetwood and do the same as I had the season before – score a shedload of goals and make people happy, me included. Leicester didn't need me. I was out of form and out of sorts and we had plenty of strikers at the club, including a young lad called Harry Kane, who'd joined on loan from Tottenham Hotspur. I'd dropped down the pecking order and needed a fresh start. But Nigel was having none of it. 'I'll see you in my office afterwards,' he said.

Craig Shakespeare and Steve Walsh, the assistant managers, were also in there when the gaffer spoke to me, and they all made it clear that I wouldn't be returning to Fleetwood now or in the future.

'You're going nowhere. You're good enough. This is where you're staying. You've got the ability and we believe in you. Work hard and you'll go on to even bigger things,' was the gist of the message.

● ● ●

It wasn't the sort of meeting I expected to be having when I stood on the pitch at the King Power Stadium back in

May 2012, holding a Leicester scarf above my head and looking around the 32,000-seater stadium that was going to be my new home. I did some interviews in the plush seats in the dugouts, where I spoke to Sky, local TV and radio, and a few newspaper reporters. Anthony Herlihy, Leicester's head of media, also interviewed me for the club website and asked what the fans should expect. I told him that I would 'always give 110 per cent and won't stop running'. I also said that I was confident I could handle jumping up three leagues, to the Championship: 'It's obviously going to be a big step, but I think that I can do it in myself. And the gaffer has been watching me, and he thinks I can do it as well.'

Little did I know what was ahead. It should have been a dream move to Leicester that summer – and, of course, it was – but there were times during that first season when I was so low that I wanted to walk away from it all. I didn't know how to handle what was happening to me and if I'd have got my way – and thankfully I didn't because Nigel and his staff had a lot more faith in me than I had in myself – I'd have been out of there.

Looking back, it was a huge leap. Being the first £1 million non-league player brought with it plenty of pressure, not so much from within the club, but certainly from outside. When Fleetwood paid Halifax £150,000 for me nine months earlier it didn't bother me in the slightest. I was moving up one league, into full-time football but still within the non-league game, and the size of the fee never crossed my mind. But Leicester was different. £1 million for someone who had never made a League appearance felt ridiculous. A few years earlier, Rotherham had been haggling with Stocksbridge over paying a couple of grand for me. Publicly, I said that the price tag didn't bother me, but privately I remember thinking that clubs were mad bidding that much – and Leicester weren't alone.

Cardiff and Peterborough also had £1 million offers accepted as the 2011–12 season drew to a close, which meant that I ended up visiting all three Championship clubs that summer before deciding where to go. John, my agent, came with me and, deep down, I think we both knew after the first meeting that I was going to sign for Leicester.

Nigel was due to go on holiday before I was scheduled to have a tour of Leicester's training ground and be introduced to his backroom staff, so he invited us to his home in Sheffield. I'd never met him before, but as a Sheffield Wednesday fan I obviously knew all about him and had gone along to see him play with my dad. He was a no nonsense centre-half, captain of the club and a Wednesday legend. In that sense, Nigel was more than just another manager to me. I respected him before I'd set foot in his house.

The only problem was that I was seeing him the day after the open-top bus parade for Fleetwood, which was never going to be a quiet affair. We were drinking on the bus and then carried on the party at the annual presentation evening at Jim's Bar, the clubhouse at the stadium. Come the end I was steaming. So, at the risk of stating the obvious, I wasn't feeling 100 per cent the next day. In fact, I was a write-off.

We ended up having a chat in Nigel's home office, where he told me how long he and his staff had been monitoring me, going right back to my time at Stocksbridge, and that he'd tried to sign me when he was in charge of Hull. He also talked about the ambition throughout the club to get promoted to the Premier League. I was impressed with everything I heard, but what I also liked was the fact that, although he knew I was going to see Peterborough and Cardiff, he didn't try to put any pressure on me to sign.

When we went to Leicester's training ground a couple of days later, it blew me away. It wasn't just the facilities, which were superb, but also the presentation that Steve Walsh, who was in charge of the club's recruitment, gave in one of the rooms upstairs. He had clips of me in action for Fleetwood, and he went through the things that had caught their eye in the games they'd come to watch. It was slick, thoughtfully put together and made me think how serious they were about signing me.

Peterborough, in comparison, were nowhere. They had a track record of bringing in non-league players and developing them, which was definitely something in their favour, but they didn't seem bothered about showing me round the stadium or the training ground. Instead, we had some food in the Wicked Witch, a restaurant that Darren Ferguson, Peterborough's manager at the time, co-owned. Barry Fry, Peterborough's director of football, was also there, and he talked finances with John downstairs while I was upstairs with Darren. We didn't stay long, probably half an hour maximum, and by the time we got in the car it was clear that Peterborough was a non-starter.

I got my head down in the passenger seat while John did the driving and woke up in south Wales, where Cardiff made much more of an effort to get me to sign. We visited their training ground at the Vale of Glamorgan, looked around Cardiff City Stadium and went out for dinner to a seafood restaurant on the marina with Malky Mackay, their manager, and Iain Moody, the head of recruitment. Cardiff, however, had one major disadvantage for me, and that was the distance to Sheffield. It would have made it almost impossible for me to see Ella, who had just turned two, and I really wanted to maintain my relationship with her. It was not as if I could get a direct flight from Cardiff to Sheffield, and sitting in a car for four-and-a-half hours would have been a nightmare. When we left I told them that I was undecided, but in my mind I couldn't see how it could possibly work at Cardiff.

So in the end Leicester came out on top, just as we thought they would at the outset. It felt like the best place to develop my career, I liked Nigel, I wasn't too far from Sheffield, and I even got an added bonus thrown in. Without me knowing, John had spoken to Nigel about the shirt number I'd like at Leicester, telling him I wanted number 9. Nigel called me out the blue – bear in mind I'd not said a word to anyone about shirt numbers – and said, 'If you want number 9, that's what you're having.' I was so thrilled that I struggled to get the words out, and just about managed to say, 'Cheers, boss.'

In the national press my transfer didn't generate a great deal of interest. Everybody in the football world was preoccupied with Chelsea playing Bayern Munich in the Champions League final, Liverpool sacking Kenny Dalglish and Roy Hodgson naming his squad for Euro 2012. There were a few lines here and there recording the fact that I'd joined Leicester, but no more than that, which suited me fine. I gave an interview to the *Leicester Mercury* in which I spoke about the belief I had in my own ability and how much I wanted to repay the faith that Nigel had shown in me.

Everything was agreed before I went off on my summer holiday, and I left all the paperwork to John, who insisted on a clause being inserted in the event of me playing for England – he was still banging that drum. In fact, that clause held up the deal for a while because I think the initial wording was 'national team' rather than England, so Andrew Neville, Leicester's football operations director, started to wonder whether I was eligible to play for another country and texted John to seek clarification. John was with me at the King Power Stadium at the time, for the photo shoot, and shouted out to ask me. 'I'm 100 per cent English!' I told him.

The new playing kit hadn't arrived at the time, so rather than wear the old one for all the photos, or my own clothes, one of the Leicester media lads grabbed some stuff from the club shop. I ended up wearing a Leicester polo shirt that looked way too big for me with a LCFC hoodie on top. Not that I was fussed. Everything felt amazing.

• • •

The three-year contract I signed was worth a basic £8,000 a week, effectively adding a zero to what I'd been earning at Fleetwood, with another £2,000 a week in the form of a loyalty payment. I was able to buy the sort of things that I'd never been able to afford before. Or, in the case of the three-bedroom penthouse apartment I moved into across the road from the King Power Stadium, rent somewhere like I'd never been able to rent before. It was a life-changing amount of money and I felt lucky to have it, but it wasn't the most important thing to me. I just wanted to play professional football.

The club put me up in the Marriott Hotel in Leicester to start with, where the cost of my accommodation was covered until I found my own place. Ritchie de Laet and Matty James joined Leicester at the same time as me, so they were staying there too and we all got on brilliantly, even if we had very different backstories. Ritchie and Matty had both arrived from Manchester United, so the contrast with me couldn't have been greater. Ritchie, a Belgian international right-back, was 23 years old, and Matty, a box-to-box midfielder who had been with United since he was 12, was 20.

After training we'd often end up in one room back at the hotel, watching *Jersey Shore* to pass the time or playing on Ritchie's PlayStation, which wouldn't work on the hotel TVs for some reason. One day Ritchie decided to do something about it, so he popped across the road to Sainsbury's and walked back through reception with a 50-inch plasma TV under his arm. I can't imagine what the hotel staff were thinking at the time.

Although I'm not shy and hadn't been fazed at all by moving to a new club when I signed for Halifax or Fleetwood, I didn't feel too sure of myself when I walked into the Leicester dressing room on the first day of preseason. People like David Nugent, Jermaine Beckford, Neil Danns and Sean St Ledger were big names to me because I'd watched them all play on TV. I was also worried about how I would measure up against players who'd been professional footballers all their lives. I certainly didn't smash the fitness work like I had previously. Put me on a 12-minute run and I'm fine. But with one of the first exercises at Leicester you had to get to various lines in a certain time – it was much more complicated than a bleep test – and I struggled. Thankfully, everyone at the club realised that I was going to take some time to adjust.

If one thing really helped me in those early days it was the relationship that I formed with 'Nuge'. He was the first person to introduce himself to me and we've never looked back since. We became so close over time that I started to think of us as brothers, and he was the obvious choice when it came to choosing a best man for my wedding. 'Nugey Pups' was what all the other lads called him.

In my eyes, Nuge had been there and done it. He started at Bury, so he knew what it was like to work his way up from the lower leagues, and he'd also played in the Premier League for Portsmouth and Burnley and, most impressively of all, worn an England shirt. He played once, against Andorra, and scored. Not a bad goal-to-game ratio for your country.

• • •

So much was new to me in professional football, but I didn't embrace everything that was pushed my way. Early in that 2012–13 season we were asked to meet with a psychologist.

I'm sure it was done with the best of intentions, but I just said, 'There's no point putting a psychologist in front of me because he won't get inside my head.'

Some of the questions seemed pointless. I was asked, 'Which two players would you have round your house for dinner?'

'Matty James and Ritchie de Laet,' I answered.

Then the psychologist said, 'Why those two?'

'Because we're stopping at the hotel together,' I replied. I seemed to be giving the same answers over and over again.

You've got to be really interested in the psychological side of the game to get something out of it, and that's just not me. Yes, I've been through dark periods and experienced moments of self-doubt, but I deal with them in my own way, not by baring my soul.

The club had a guy who used to hypnotise some of the lads, and they'd talk about how it would hopefully help them score more goals. I was thinking, Are you fucking mad? I'll tell you how you score more goals – go out on the training field and practise your shooting.

It wasn't that long before I started to be myself at Leicester – which meant having plenty to say in the dressing room. It was a close-knit and down-to-earth group, which helped with the bedding-in process. Nigel was building a strong team – Danny Drinkwater, Matty James, Andy King, Wes Morgan, Jeffrey Schlupp, Kasper Schmeichel and Ritchie de Laet were all part of the squad back then – with a view not only to winning promotion, but also being able to compete once we were in the Premier League. I couldn't wait to get started.

My Leicester career got underway against Torquay United on 14 August 2012, a Tuesday night at Plainmoor in the sort of low-key surroundings that I'd been used to playing in for Fleetwood. It was a Capital One Cup first-round tie played in front of 3,367, and I headed in Ben Marshall's cross after 77 minutes to mark my debut with a goal. I should have had a second but another header was ruled out for offside – I was gutted about it at the time. Still, we won 4–0 and I'd got off the mark, so there was plenty to be happy about. I got my first league goal 11 days later in a 2–1 defeat at Blackburn Rovers.

A week after losing at Blackburn we beat Blackpool 1–0 at home, ending their 100 per cent record, but it's a match that I remember for all the wrong reasons. Ian Holloway, who had paid me all those compliments at the start of the year when I played against Blackpool in the FA Cup for Fleetwood, accused me of 'blatantly diving' to win the penalty that decided the game, even though Tiago Gomes jumped in. Much worse than that, though, was the shocking abuse I received on social media from some Blackpool fans, who targeted not only me, but also Ella. Having someone say that they hope you and your daughter die of AIDS is not particularly pleasant. The next day the Blackpool Supporters' Association condemned those responsible for the tweets, and one of the people at the centre of it apologised to me and sent a letter to the club, so I decided to let it be.

It was another example of the way my world had changed now that I was no longer a non-league footballer. I had suddenly gained loads more Twitter followers, so I had to be careful with what I said on social media. Anything that happened on the pitch was replayed over and over again on Sky Sports News. I was running out in front of 25,000 people in the Championship instead of a crowd in the hundreds at some non-league clubs. And I knew I couldn't get away with telling Leicester's media team that I was worth £20 a week and a packet of Maltesers, which is what I came out with at Halifax one day. Everything was under so much more scrutiny than before, and with that came a level of expectation that was totally new to me.

At the same time, I hadn't forgotten where I'd come from. In the first international break, in September, I went to watch Fleetwood play at Morecambe. Andy Mangan spotted me in the crowd and ran over to celebrate one of their goals with me as I leant over the advertising hoarding for a man hug.

The following month, I treated my mates to a night out to celebrate my move to Leicester. I arranged for about 20 of us to go to the greyhound track at Owlerton Stadium, near Hillsborough, where we had a hospitality suite for the night.

It worked out even better because England were playing San Marino that evening in a World Cup 2014 qualifier, so we could watch that on the TV in the background. When the waitress came in to order the drinks I thought it could take a while, so I asked if I could buy the fridge. I also requested five bottles of Grey Goose vodka, but they only had four on site, so the waitress apologised and we made do. By the end of the evening England had won 5–0, my mates were singing San Marino songs and the fridge was empty.

* * *

In those first couple of months at Leicester I wasn't exactly setting it alight on the pitch, but things were going along OK. We beat Burnley 2–1 at home and I got the winner, which was my first goal at the King Power Stadium, and at the end of September I scored again, this time the equaliser in a 2–1 victory at Middlesbrough, to make it four in nine appearances. But then the wheels came off. I went nine games without scoring, and one of the staff got an insight into the way I was living my life away from football. Perhaps they'd already guessed, but the proof was in the pudding – well, actually in my bloodstream – after Yannick Bolasie kicked me on my calf in a 2–1 home defeat to Crystal Palace on 27 October. I had a dead leg, which is a fairly routine injury, but it was taking an age to get better.

Around that time I had a three-litre vodka bottle at home that I would put loads and loads of Skittles in. Once one batch of Skittles had fully dissolved, I'd top it up with more, but with one important condition – I'd only put the red or purple sweets in, because when I eat them I don't fancy the orange, green and yellow ones. I kept repeating the process, and I must have put a different batch of Skittles in at least 20 times. After that, you can drink the vodka neat and it tastes just like Skittles, so you don't get that minging taste. When I was feeling bored at home in the evening I'd pour myself a glass, sit back and enjoy.

The vodka was decent but it turned out that it wasn't doing much for my dead leg, which didn't stop bleeding for ages. Dave Rennie, the physio, said that he couldn't believe it wasn't improving – he'd seen a torn calf muscle heal quicker. He pulled me aside one day when nobody else was about.

'What are you doing?' Dave said.

'Nothing that I wouldn't normally do,' I replied. Then I explained that what I'd normally do was drink Skittle vodka.

'Well, that will be why, then,' Dave said, looking a little shocked, before going on to explain the science behind it and how the alcohol was damaging the healing process.

Three weeks later I returned to action as a first-half substitute in a 6–0 win over Ipswich, and the following Saturday I was back in the starting lineup to face Sheffield Wednesday at

Hillsborough. We won 2–0 but I didn't get among the goals, and it was not until 8 December, when I came off the bench to get a 90th minute equaliser in a 2–2 draw against Barnsley, that I scored again. It turned out to be my fifth and final goal of the 2012–13 season.

Nigel supported me the whole time – that's the type of manager he is, almost like a surrogate father to his players and never the sort to publicly criticise – but behind the scenes people knew that I was doing myself no favours and my lifestyle, in particular my drinking, was a problem. I got on a downer because the season wasn't following the pattern of previous years, when I was used to scoring loads and being the main man, and my way of dealing with that was to go and get pissed with my mates back in Sheffield. It was a way of escaping.

If we played Saturday and then had the Sunday off, I'd drive back home and go out on the Saturday night, and if we were off on the Wednesday I'd probably go out on the Tuesday night, either in Leicester or in the Viper Rooms in Sheffield for their Risqué night. As always, whenever I went out it was all or nothing, so leaving time was closing time.

My sleep pattern was screwed. I'd invite friends over to the apartment and sometimes wouldn't go to bed until 3 or 4am. When I got home from training I was knackered. If I put a film on I'd be asleep before the opening scene had finished. Other days, I'd climb straight into bed in the afternoon. Maybe my body wasn't used to the intensity of it all – Leicester was a massive gear change from what I was used to at Fleetwood. That siesta would turn into a full-on kip, and there were times when I wouldn't wake up until 6 or 7pm. The knock-on effect was that I'd be wired at 3am.

I didn't have a girlfriend at the time and, looking back, there wasn't a lot of structure to my life other than getting to see Ella a few times a month. My parents would often bring her down to Leicester with them if we were playing at home. Ella would come to the game, stay over at my apartment and I'd take her back to Sheffield on the Sunday after having some time with her.

For a lot of the time, though, I was on my own, and that led to boredom. Sometimes I'd be at a loose end and head over to the Soar Point, a student pub in the heart of the university campus only a couple of minutes from my place in Leicester. I'd be able to go there and have something to eat and a few drinks without getting hassled, thanks probably to the fact that most of the people in there were students. I'd go in there on a Wednesday if we had the day off, and sometimes I'd drop by on a Sunday to watch the live football.

You were entitled to a discount in the Soar Point if you had a yellow student card. I obviously didn't qualify for one or need one, but the manager of the pub insisted, so that knocked a bit more money off the drinks. They were only about £1.50 in the first place. I had some proper sessions in there. They used to do a night with a stock exchange theme, where drinks would flash up on a big screen as if you were trading in the city. If someone had just been to the bar and bought four pints of Carling, that would put the price of Carling up on the screen, and that was what you would pay if you went to the bar. Naturally, my mates and I would buy whichever was the cheapest.

That January I had a big party at my apartment to celebrate my 26th birthday. I invited about 30 people and went to Costco beforehand to stock up on booze. I also bought a load of fireworks – I've no idea what I was thinking of there. Come the end of the evening, rockets were being launched into the sky and eggs towards the ground from the balcony. I doubt the neighbours approved, but Mario Balotelli would probably have been proud of me.

Clearly, there were times when I wasn't concentrating on football that season and I went off the rails. I won't try to pretend otherwise. But I wasn't drinking every day, as has been suggested, and I don't remember the conversation with Aiyawatt Srivaddhanaprabha ('Top'), our vice-chairman and someone I have a lot of respect for, about needing to change my lifestyle. I think he must be confusing me with someone else, especially when he said that I quit drinking after he had a chat with me.

There were certainly days when I turned up for training smelling of booze after my move from Fleetwood, but it wasn't a regular thing. On one occasion, Walshy and Shakey, Nigel's assistants, knew that I'd come in after a night out and they spoke to my agent about it. John was already aware of what was going on – he'd been telling me to knuckle down for a while – but he also explained to the club that I was in a bad place and I needed an arm around me, which was true, even if some of my problems were self-inflicted.

I wasn't used to experiencing setbacks on the pitch, and I'd never had so much money in my life before, which allowed me to escape from things without any financial consequences. I'd scored twenty-plus goals year on year, pretty much ever since I joined Stocksbridge, and all of a sudden I was stuck on five. Falling short like that was tough for me, and as I tried to get my head around everything that was going on I came to what I saw as the logical conclusion: This level is obviously not for me.

It wasn't like me to doubt myself but, for a while, I was convinced that I wasn't good enough to play in the Championship. I found adapting to the standard really hard, especially in such a short space of time. I couldn't give defenders a ten-yard headstart and outpace them any more, my runs had to be much more intelligent because of the positioning and ability of the players I was up against, and the way I had lived my life previously was obviously not the thing to do now that I was a professional footballer.

I'm sure my teammates knew that I was pissing it up. Some of them were probably doing it as well, but they knew when and how often to do it – that was the big difference. I'd never had that mindset. In non-league football I could have a night out, play the next day and coast through the game, just like I did on New Year's Day at Goole. That seemed like a long time ago now.

There were the crowds to get used to as well. Playing in front of so many people was great when it was going your way, but it wasn't much fun when you were getting stick. Nigel said a few years later that he could tell that sections of the Leicester supporters doubted I had the ability to make the step up. In other words, they weren't having me. I could sense that as well. I'm not stupid. As much as you try to shut out the background noise, you can hear the moans and groans when something goes wrong on the pitch in just the same way that you feed off the buzz when they're singing your name.

Maybe it was easy for some people to write me off at Leicester. After all, I'd spent nine years in non-league football and there was no track record of success at Championship level. My lack of goals only confirmed what the doubters had suspected before I'd kicked a ball.

One of the mistakes I made was to take far too much notice of what was being said on social media. People don't hold back with their criticism, which was fine when I was playing out of my skin for Fleetwood and everyone was writing positive stuff, but a totally different kettle of fish when I was coming up short at Leicester. When I looked through the notifications on my Twitter account – something that footballers should never do – and came across comments from people saying that I wasn't good enough, and that the club had wasted £1 million and should have signed someone else, it hurt me. Ultimately, it was my fault for reading them, and I wasn't doing enough to prove people wrong. But it started to feel like I was caught up in a vicious circle, and I couldn't see a way out.

In February that season, after a run of three straight defeats, Harry Kane arrived from Spurs. He was only 19 and we hardly played together during his three months at the club. Chris Wood had signed from West Brom in January and was on fire from the off, so I spent a lot of time watching games from the substitutes' bench, which was something that had never happened to me before.

I didn't know what to do. I was confused and capable of coming out with anything, including that remark to a few teammates that I was thinking about becoming a rep in Ibiza. Looking back, I seemed to have a habit of throwing Ibiza into conversations, with the Halifax end-of-season interview as well, probably because I went there in 2007 with Stocksbridge reserves and in 2008 with my mates, and it represented non-stop partying in my eyes. I'd been happy there – and I wanted to feel happy again.

● ● ●

In fairness, I wasn't the only person struggling at Leicester in the second half of the 2012–13 season. After being second in the table at the end of January and targeting automatic promotion, the team fell away and we were clinging onto a play-off place come the middle of March, after a run of five games without a win. There was an international break that month, so Nigel decided that it was time to escape and he took us away to Portugal for a warm-weather training camp. We trained, spent a bit of time go-karting, went out for a meal together at a restaurant one evening and, in an activity that didn't appear on any itinerary, four of us ended up face-down on the tarmac with guns pointed at our heads.

It was the night before we were due to fly home and a group of us decided to sneak out. We were staying in two-bedroom apartments, almost like chalets, and we couldn't go out the front way because we'd be seen by the management staff, so we scaled a fence at the back. We walked quite far until a taxi picked us up and took us into the town centre, where we had a few drinks. When it was time to go back, I got in the front of a cab and waited for the lads to get in. All of a sudden, the taxi driver said, 'No. Trouble. Get out.' I didn't know what he was on about. He said, 'Your friends!' I looked in the mirror and they were all running up the road. I got out the car and the next thing I heard was, *Bang, bang, bang*. It was a gun going off.

I ran towards the boys, who were having a little scuffle with a few locals. We got away, went down a few side streets and managed to find the main road, where we thought we could get back to the hotel. We needed to anyway – it was starting to get light and we had a plane to catch. The next minute, sirens were going off. Two police cars pulled up, and the coppers jumped out, pointing guns at us and telling us to get down on the floor. We did as we were told – even I know to keep my mouth shut when someone's holding a gun.

One of the police officers tried to talk to us, but none of us knew what he was saying. After plenty of miscommunication – including a moment when I thought, *What the fuck?* as one lad pleaded with the coppers to go easy because he was married and had two watches – we just about managed to get our story across. It turned out that the gunshots we'd heard had come from a fake gun one of the locals was carrying, although it sounded real enough.

With that, we were told to go back to the hotel – though not before we asked the police officer which way we had to go. We sneaked in and got some kip before we got the plane home – all as if nothing had happened.

Unfortunately, the Portuguese sunshine did nothing for our form on the pitch. We failed to win any of the next four matches and ended up scraping into the play-offs on the final day of the season after beating Nottingham Forest 3–2. We played Watford in the play-off semi-finals. I never got on in either game, and the second leg at Vicarage Road, where I was on the bench with Harry Kane and Drinky, turned into a horrible day. With the score 2–2 on aggregate, we were awarded a penalty deep into injury-time after Anthony Knockaert was brought down. Knockaert was not the regular penalty taker – Nuge would normally have stepped up – but he got the ball and was adamant that he was going to score. His kick was saved, and 20 seconds later the ball was in the back of our net.

It was chaos at the end. All the Watford fans were running everywhere, going mental, and we couldn't get down the tunnel quickly enough. We'd blown it – not just that afternoon, but that season.

Everyone would have a point to prove when we reported back, but no one more so than me. I had in my mind that chat with Nigel, Walshy and Shakey, which was probably the best thing that happened to me, because I needed to know that they still believed in me. I was determined not to let them down.

7

THE PROPOSAL

We were in La Rocca, a nightclub on the fringes of Antwerp, in Belgium, and I could feel another dropped beer bottle crunching under my feet. It was about two o'clock in the morning, far too much alcohol had been consumed and I was hatching a plan with Ritchie de Laet about what was going to happen next.

There were more romantic places for what I had in mind, for sure, but something told me – and it was totally off the cuff, so I can't begin to explain why it came into my head – that this was the moment. Only a week or so earlier we'd been away with Matty James and his fiancée, Leah, and I'd told Becky that marriage had never interested me.

Ritchie, who'd invited us over to his home city for the weekend to spend some time with him and his wife, Thane, told Becky that I wanted to speak to her. Sober and tired, she wasn't really in the mood for any more of our antics. We'd spent a fortune buying overpriced champagne, for no other reason than the Albanians sitting close by were drinking massive bottles of vodka and we wanted to try to compete with them. Not that they seemed to pay any attention to us.

Becky didn't seem impressed with my request and told Ritchie that I should go to her if I had something to say. So I got up from the table, stumbled over to the other side of the room and, on a carpet of broken glass and booze, got down on one knee. 'I never thought I'd be doing this, but will you marry me?' I said.

There was no engagement ring – that would have to wait – and for a while Becky seemed convinced that I didn't mean a word of it because I was drunk. But after getting to my feet and threatening to put on a repeat performance, she eventually gave in. 'Yes, I will,' she said, smiling and suspecting that I'd never remember any of it when I woke up in the morning.

It was 15 June 2014, less than 24 hours after we'd sat in a beach bar watching England lose 2–1 against Italy in their opening World Cup match in Brazil and, more importantly, only five months after I'd met Becky, when she had the misfortune of organising my 27th birthday party.

* * *

Becky Nicholson was the events manager at the Viper Rooms, where I was having my party. I'd been exchanging messages with her for a while about exactly what we wanted. Plenty of alcohol was the short answer. Well, and a load of laughing gas balloons stapled to a wall, at the request of the Inbetweeners.

Becky agreed to everything but wished she hadn't when she spent an entire day sitting on the floor filling up 250 balloons from a nitrous-oxide tank. By the time she'd finished, she had cuts all over her fingers, and she sent me a text to say that she was pretty pissed off. When we rocked up, with a few beers already on board, her day didn't get any better.

She didn't disappoint us in the drinks department, however, laying on something the club called the 'Glamour & Excess Luxurious Chest, Perpetual Indulgence and Immoderation', to quote its full title. It contained, in no particular order, Courvoisier VS, peach schnapps, Gosling's, Wray & Nephew, Havana Club 7, Bacardi Superior and Pampero Especial, topped with two bottles of Moët & Chandon. On the marketing blurb it said: 'Served for eight in a real treasure chest'. I got through virtually the lot myself within an hour of walking into the club. I wasn't even putting it in a glass – I was just dipping my head in.

My birthday party was the day after we'd beaten Derby County 4–1 at the King Power Stadium to go seven points clear at the top of the Championship. I'd scored my eighth goal of the season in what turned out to be our best performance of the campaign. Derby were also going for promotion at the time, but it felt like men against boys that Friday evening as we took them apart. We were still on a high when we met up the next day.

Along with the Inbetweeners and a load of other friends from Sheffield, quite a few of the Leicester lads came out that night, including Wes Morgan, Danny Drinkwater and Matty James, who had all become good mates. Drinky, like Jamo, had come through at Manchester United, and he joined Leicester around the same time as Wes, in early 2012. You could see that he'd been schooled at United because he had such high standards on the pitch, in particular when it came to what he expected from himself. As for Wes, he's impossible not to like. He's one of those skippers who leads by example, rather than ranting and raving, and has an easy-going and laid-back personality off the field. I've got a vision of him on that January evening – and it's a hazy memory – strolling round the club with a bottle of champagne in his hand, toasting my birthday and our lead at the top of the Championship table.

I got the impression – and it was only an impression because I was too pissed to know for sure – that Becky wasn't that chuffed with how we behaved that night. Particularly me. After working my way through the treasure chest I was no use to anyone. One of the lads spotted me swaying in the toilets and decided that it was in everyone's interests if I was packed off in a taxi to a hotel that was only a two-minute walk away. I started to come round in the hotel room, where I bombarded Becky with messages saying how much I liked her. She blanked every one of them, which wasn't surprising in the circumstances.

Waking up worse for wear the next morning, I decided that there was only one thing for it: hair of the dog. Nigel had given us Saturday, Sunday and Monday off as a reward for that win over Derby, so, as I'd tried to focus a bit more on my football that season, I saw it as a good reason to have a proper blow-out across the weekend – something I'd normally only do in the summer. I met up with my mates in Hillsborough for another session on Sunday, and in between drinks I was constantly texting Becky, apologising for how drunk I was the night before and trying to talk her into meeting up.

I was single at the time and had been ever since Emma and I had gone our separate ways before Ella was born. The idea of settling down wasn't something that particularly interested me because I enjoyed my freedom and independence, but I couldn't get Becky out of my head and I wasn't going to give up. Eventually, on Monday, there was a breakthrough. She agreed to meet me, although the terms weren't that encouraging. 'I'll come and see you just because you're pestering me so much that I want to tell you to stop texting,' she said. I wasn't sure whether she was joking or not.

The plan was to have a quiet day on Monday, but Grant, one of the Inbetweeners, talked me into going to see him at the Castle Inn in Hillsborough for a drink. I asked for a J_2O because I was training the next day, but Grant returned from the bar with double vodkas. By the time Becky turned up I was several drinks down, enjoying a game of pool and brazen enough to wrap my arms around her when she walked through the door. The next thing she knew, I was on the floor wrestling with one of my mates. It was going to go one of two ways at that point, and thankfully Becky saw the funny side. Despite declining my offer of a glass of wine, she decided to hang around. Come the end of the evening, we were getting on well and having a good laugh together. Somehow I'd managed to rescue the situation.

The next day I was back at training and, not surprisingly, feeling horrendous. One of my mates had to drive my car down to Leicester, and it didn't take long for the gaffer to work out what had gone on over the weekend. I didn't stop running in training, trying to sweat out all the alcohol, but the clues must have been there because as we walked off the pitch towards the changing room at the end of the session, Nigel glanced across at me and said, 'Well, looks like someone enjoyed their birthday.'

I just smiled a bit awkwardly. In some ways I'd changed from the player who'd gone off the rails in the first season – on the pitch things were a hundred times better – but I was still living the good life.

• • •

A trip to Magaluf in the summer of 2013 probably wasn't the ideal place to get everything back on track after that gut-wrenching defeat at Watford and all the other problems that accompanied my first season as a professional footballer, but I needed a change of scenery. My old housemate Rob Atkinson provided it when he invited me along to his stag-do, and as luck would have it Fleetwood were out there at the same time on their end-of-season tour.

I've been to Magaluf a few times, including one memorable holiday with the Inbetweeners, which ended with one of them going home with a permanent reminder of me on his backside. We were in a bar one night, just chilling out, when we saw a tattoo shop across the road. Rans looked at me and said, 'I'm going to get your signature tattooed on my arse.'

'Don't be stupid,' I replied.

'I'm serious,' he said.

'Go and find out how much it'll cost and I'll pay for it,' I said.

Like an idiot, he got them to agree to do it – for 30 euros. I signed my name on a scrap of paper, handed over the money and Rans, looking pleased with himself, got it done there and then. He's got my autograph on his arse for life now.

I didn't set foot in the tattoo shop on this latest trip to Magaluf, but I couldn't leave the punching machine alone. Whenever I went missing for a bit, the lads knew that they'd find me trying to knock seven bells out of it. I've always enjoyed having a go on them, although the machine ended up getting the better of me. One night I got a bit carried away, followed through with a punch and connected with the machine itself, breaking a couple of bones in my hand in the process. And that's why I started the 2013–14 season with my hand strapped up.

Before returning for preseason I went on another holiday, to Zante in Greece, where I did the sort of fitness work that I'd never felt the need to in the past – that's how much I wanted to get off to a flyer when I returned to training with Leicester. Most people were in Zante for a massive piss-up – and don't get me wrong, I had a few drinks myself – but I got into decent shape after becoming friendly with the hotel owner, who'd seen me play on TV. He took me out one morning to show me a good place to go for a run, and I did it every day, going flat-out in the blazing sunshine and then jumping straight into the pool when I got back.

It all paid off, because when the season got underway I felt back to being the old me – sharp and aggressive – and was determined to put the previous 12 months behind me. Nigel must have recognised that as well, because he picked me in his starting 11 on the opening day – for the first time since February – and I got the winning goal in a 2–1 victory at Middlesbrough. Drinky also scored, and we both celebrated by cupping our ears in front of our own fans, who'd been giving us a bit of stick because of our performances the season before.

At the start of that season I made some changes to my pre-match routine, and it's remained the same to this day. With a traditional three o'clock Saturday kick-off, I'll have a can of Red Bull as soon as I wake up, which is gone in 30 seconds. I don't have breakfast and won't eat anything until I have a cheese-and-ham omelette with baked beans at half-eleven. I wash that down with another Red Bull, which I also neck quickly. While we're waiting around and killing a bit of time, I have a double espresso, normally with centre-half Marcin Wasilewski, a cracking bloke who trains as hard as he plays.

We get into the dressing room an hour and a half before kick-off, and I'll have a third can of Red Bull straight away, but with this one I sip it all the way until we go out for the warm-up, leaving a bit to finish off when I come back in. So three Red Bulls, a double espresso and a cheese-and-ham omelette is what makes me run around like a nutjob on a match day.

At Middlesbrough, Nuge came off the bench to set up my goal in a sign of things to come that season. We formed a fantastic partnership together that mirrored how well we got on off the pitch. We were like two peas in a pod. We knew each other's game inside out, complemented each other because we were so different in our style of play, and it soon felt like everything we did came off.

I was always on the move, looking to run in behind, while Nuge seemed to play at his own pace, sometimes chatting away and smiling while the game was going on. He made us all chuckle that season with something he did at Loftus Road in December, when the game was held up for four minutes because there was a squirrel on the pitch. The fans were singing, 'Squirrel, there's only one squirrel,' and the linesman just stood there looking at it, not sure what to do. Nuge grabbed the bull by the horns, or maybe that should be the squirrel by the tail, and started chasing it across the pitch. He was laughing his head off while running after it, before the ground staff eventually intervened.

Although I got the winner that day against QPR, Nuge was leading the way in the goalscoring charts and I couldn't have been happier for him. That victory was the start of a run of nine straight league wins. The team was flying and I was full of confidence, with all those doubts that had plagued me the previous season now a distant memory. I couldn't wait to play every week, and I found it really frustrating when I had to sit out the New Year's Day trip to Millwall through suspension after I picked up my fifth booking of the season against Bolton.

I was annoyed because it was the last match before the yellow cards got wiped, and I also felt that I did nothing wrong to get the booking. I jumped up for a header with Zat Knight, the Bolton centre-half who is six-foot-seven and a bit of a man mountain, and as I came down I landed on top of his foot. It was totally accidental but he thought I did it on purpose, so he grabbed me by the throat and we started arguing. 'You'd better back down,' he said.

It was like being back in the non-league days for a moment. 'You've got no fucking chance,' I replied. We were both shouting at each other, and the referee came over, spoke to the linesman and decided to book us both.

With the January transfer window open, the gaffer brought in a couple of new signings to strengthen the squad for the second half of the season. One of them was Kevin Phillips, who was a legend in my eyes because of all the goals he'd scored at the highest level. I don't think any of us had heard of the other lad, whose name was Riyad Mahrez. Walshy, on one of his many scouting trips, discovered Riyad playing for Le Havre in the French second division. Riyad was wiry but deceptively strong, and we knew that he had the potential to be something special as soon as we saw him in training. He had some unbelievable tricks and this ability to just slip past players.

Kev, on the other hand, had been there and done it and needed no introduction. He'd played for Sunderland,

Southampton, Aston Villa, Birmingham and Crystal Palace in the Premier League, scoring goals pretty much wherever he went, and also represented England, so straight away I saw him as someone I could learn from. Kev was 40 when he joined – I remember him celebrating a late winner at Bournemouth by pretending that he had a walking stick – and come the end of the season he would decide to hang up his boots and take up a coaching position at Leicester. As a player and a coach he was a huge help to me, teaching me about the runs I should be making and what type of finish to try in a certain position.

In the early part of 2014 we were running away with the league and I was playing my best football in a Leicester shirt. The goal I scored in the 2–1 win against Birmingham at the end of January was my tenth of the season, doubling my tally from my first year, and I felt as though I'd completely turned it around and belonged at that level.

• • •

I was spending quite a bit of time with Becky by this stage, but winning her over was taking a while. She wasn't easily persuaded but I just kept chipping away, refusing to take no for an answer. She was five years older than me, lived in Barnsley and had two children – Megan, who was eight, and Taylor, who was four – from previous relationships. Obviously, I was in a similar position with Ella, so we were on the same wavelength in that sense, which probably helped. We started going out on a few dates and we became closer, but I hadn't put the brakes on my social life and was still going out with my mates, so I stupidly thought nothing of not replying to messages or calls from Becky for several days. At times I was like a plane that had disappeared off radar and, unsurprisingly, it started to drive Becky mad.

One night I pushed it too far when we were supposed to be going out and I didn't turn up or answer the phone. Finally, I rang Becky back the next day, but she had already decided to come to my apartment in Leicester to see me. She turned up absolutely raging. I was standing in the kitchen and she threw a book at me. She was so angry – and she'd been calling me so many times because she'd been trying to tell me something. I had no idea what was coming ... and then she said it. She was pregnant.

I didn't know what to say. I liked Becky in a way that I couldn't remember feeling about anyone before, but we'd only known each other a couple of months and we weren't officially together. I couldn't really take it all in.

Once everything calmed down a bit we had a proper chat, and not just about the pregnancy. Becky felt that I needed to change my lifestyle, for myself as much as anyone. She'd seen things that maybe I didn't want to see and that are perhaps easier to recognise when you're an outsider looking in, and that conversation continued over the following weeks, after we'd decided to make a proper go of things together.

Becky recognised that I had some genuine mates, people who were with me for the right reasons, but she thought that four or five others were hangers on, taking advantage of me. I didn't see it like that at first and we had a bit of an argument about it. Becky pointed out that I'd pay for everything on a night out, and she questioned whether some of the people would still be my friends if I wasn't putting my hand in my pocket all the time. In my eyes that was just me being me. I wasn't being flash. I was just sharing what I was fortunate to be earning, maybe being a bit overly generous sometimes.

I know that Becky found it difficult to have that discussion. She didn't want it to come across as if she was trying to manipulate me or control any aspect of my life, yet I think she was also worried that if she didn't say anything my world would have caved in.

There were other things that she couldn't get her head around, like my diet. I'd often get bored in the apartment, invite some mates over to get on the PlayStation or watch football on the TV, and inevitably we'd end up eating rubbish. I love a pizza, and Domino's may as well have been on speed dial in those first two seasons at Leicester.

I was living on my own and I could never be bothered to cook anything. I also knew – and this used to drive some of my

Leicester teammates mad – that I could eat whatever I wanted and, in terms of my physique, it wouldn't affect me in the slightest. I'd never go in the gym, because I was naturally fit and I couldn't see any value in putting on muscle that would only slow me down. Weight-wise, I've always been between 72 and 74 kilograms, and my body fat is 5 to 6 per cent no matter what I do. I'm just very lucky in this respect. Kasper Schmeichel would do his nut about it whenever he saw me snacking on something unhealthy because he's one of those people who has to watch everything he eats.

Doing everything by the book has never been my style. When I joined Leicester I started using snus, which are nicotine pouches that you place against your gums for ten minutes or so. I used to have the odd fag on a night out at Fleetwood, but one of the lads introduced me to snus when I first signed for Leicester and I found that they helped me to chill out. Leicester knew from the outset. A lot more footballers use them than people realise, and some lads even play with them in during matches.

I didn't turn a deaf ear to everything Becky said, because I knew there was a degree of truth to it all. But it wasn't going to be a case of flicking a switch and everything changing overnight. That only happened when we moved in together in June, when I realised and accepted that I needed to get control of things.

• • •

On the pitch, everything was continuing to go to plan. I got two in a 3–0 win at Barnsley, scoring for the fourth game in succession, and 11 days later I converted Ritchie de Laet's cross to register my 16th of the season in a 1–1 draw at Blackburn. We were unbeaten in 17 matches, five points clear of Burnley in second place and, while there was no hint of any complacency inside the club, it felt like a matter of when, not if, we would be promoted to the Premier League.

That moment arrived a fortnight later, when QPR lost at Bournemouth and Derby failed to win at Middlesbrough. Leicester were back in the top-flight after a ten-year absence. We'd beaten Sheffield Wednesday the night before, so a lot of the lads went round to Andy King's apartment on the Saturday afternoon to watch the results come in, before meeting up later that evening to celebrate.

It was a huge achievement for everyone at the club, and I really believe that what happened the previous season, when everything unravelled so badly and we suffered that cruel defeat at Vicarage Road in the play-offs, pulled everyone closer together and gave us the extra motivation to do what we did.

There were still another six games remaining, but I played in just one of them – a 1–1 draw at Reading – and lasted only 65 minutes after suffering a recurrence of a groin problem that had surfaced a few weeks earlier. I went for a scan and they couldn't see anything, so Dave Rennie, the physio, arranged for me to see a guy called David Lloyd, a consultant surgeon in Leicester who specialises in groin pain in elite athletes. He identified something really tiny, in my iliacus, a pair of muscles deep inside the pelvic area. He had to give me a horrible injection, and I watched on a screen as this huge needle, about six inches long, disappeared into my groin. He hit the spot and I saw the liquid coming out.

While the season was over for me, the lads still had the title to wrap up. A 1–0 win at Bolton did the job, thanks to a right-foot rocket from Lloyd Dyer. When the final game of the season approached, when we would be presented with the trophy, I sensed an opportunity for Skittle vodka to make a public appearance. I had one that had been brewing nicely for the best part of six months with promotion in mind, and I dread to think how many Skittles had dissolved in there over that time.

Once we'd finished the ceremony on the pitch, collected our medals and walked around with our families, the gaffer asked everyone to come into the dressing room, where we had a celebration among ourselves before going upstairs to join the directors and the rest of the staff at the club. It was then that I produced the Skittle vodka, poured it into one of those huge water containers and shared it round with everyone. It was really sweet and almost like a syrup, but it went down a treat. Even the gaffer seemed to enjoy it.

A few days before that I'd picked up the players' player of the year trophy at the club's annual awards dinner – an evening that was a lot more enjoyable than 12 months earlier, and not just because things had worked out so differently on the pitch.

At Leicester, people can buy a table for the dinner and sit with a couple of the players. But in my first year, the bloke who paid for the table I was on with Andy King couldn't make it, so he gave it to his son, who was a student and invited all his university mates. As a punter at the Soar Point I hardly had a problem with that, but our season hadn't ended and it was a long evening drinking Twinings flavoured tea – cranberry and blood orange, if I remember right – with Kingy while the students ordered another eight pints every time the waitress came near the table. They were steaming before long, and we just wanted to get out of there.

I've always got on well with Kingy – he's the ultimate pro and one of those lads you'll never hear anyone say a bad word about because he just quietly gets on with his job – so we sat together again the second year, but this time I had a guy called Elio Buizza alongside me too, and we hit it off straight away. Elio runs a multinational company that designs shops. He's such a lovely bloke and we became really close friends, to the point that Becky and I would ask him to be our daughter's godfather.

We still had two more official functions before the close-season break. The first was an open-top bus parade that finished with us being introduced one by one to all the supporters at the town hall, and the second involved an amazing trip to Thailand, courtesy of Vichai Srivaddhanaprabha, Leicester's owner. On both occasions I risked getting into a bit of bother over hats. Outside the town hall I asked a copper if I could borrow his helmet, and I scarpered up the stairs with it on my head before he had chance to answer, and in Thailand I upset Andrew Neville, Leicester's football operations director, by throwing his cap into the sea.

In Phuket, we set off on a boat to visit a little island where they put water sports on for all the players and staff, and I swiped the cap off Andrew's head and flicked it into the water. It was only supposed to be a bit of fun – one of those things that I do without thinking – but Andrew went mad. It turned out that he'd climbed Mount Kilimanjaro with that hat on, so it had special significance to him, and he didn't appreciate the sight of it bobbing along in the sea as our boat headed in the opposite direction. Needless to say, I felt pretty bad afterwards.

We spent seven days in Thailand and it was an incredible experience. Vichai, who has been Leicester's owner since 2010, and 'Top', his son, could not have made us feel more welcome in their country. Whether visiting temples, releasing sea turtles into the wild or having our pictures taken with tiger cubs, we did something different every day. We also had a fantastic meal in Sirocco, a restaurant on the 63rd floor of the State Tower in Bangkok that looks out on the whole of the city and features in the film *The Hangover Part II*. It was completely shut off just for us – that's how well we were looked after – and the views were absolutely stunning.

As much as I was enjoying myself in Thailand, Becky was tearing her hair out back home because she was thoroughly fed up with being unable to get hold of me. I've never been one for long phone calls when a text message will do, but this was obviously different because she was now my girlfriend and pregnant with our child. Being in a relationship was new to me, so it took some time to adjust, but I can also see how frustrating it must have been for Becky when I did yet another vanishing act.

The situation reached breaking point after we got back from Thailand. We had six weeks off in the summer, and I stayed at Becky's house one night. I got up the next morning to go to see my mates in Sheffield for a few drinks and I went AWOL for the weekend. My phone was in my pocket but I wouldn't bother looking at it, and it was often out of battery anyway, so there was no way anyone could track me down.

Wise to my ways by now, Becky knew that I would be in one of three places: Champs, the sports bar that had replaced the Yew Tree Inn, near where I grew up; the Malin Bridge Inn around the corner; or the Castle Inn, in Hillsborough. Becky found me in Champs, where I was pissed and surrounded by my mates, as well as some people she didn't think were a good influence on me. She was emotional and, in front of everyone, told me that she couldn't take it any more.

'I'm not going to bring a child into your crazy world if you continue to behave this way,' she said, and with that, she walked out.

We didn't speak for a couple of days, despite my best efforts to make contact. I was getting a taste of my own medicine, and I had no option but to drive to Barnsley to try to salvage things. We were chatting in her kitchen and I got emotional, which is not like me, but the reality of the situation had dawned on me. I knew that Becky was ready to walk away, and I really didn't want to contemplate losing her, so I listened to what she had to say.

'There are people out there who would die to be in your position,' she said. 'You've got the whole world at your feet. Make something of your life, whether it's with me or someone else. But don't throw it away.'

Maybe I'd wanted to have the best of both worlds – a beautiful girlfriend and a single life that allowed me to meet up with the lads whenever and wherever I wanted – but something had to give, and I wasn't going to let Becky slip through my fingers. I told her that she was the one, that I never wanted to be with anyone else – and I promised I'd change. Looking back now, that was the defining weekend in our relationship, and committing to Becky was the best decision I ever made.

A little while afterwards we went out to see Ritchie and Thane in Antwerp, and by the end of June we'd moved into our own place in Mountsorrel, a village in Leicestershire on the River Soar, where I'd take Megan and Taylor down to the river bank and teach them how to fish, just like my granddad had with me when I was younger. Life was no longer a hundred miles an hour and, with a baby on the way, an engagement ring to buy and Premier League football on the horizon, the future could not have been brighter.

8

GREAT ESCAPE

'That fucking goose.'

In the summer of 2014 I lost count of the number of times we muttered those words while rubbing our eyes in the middle of another night of interrupted sleep and cursing the bloody bird that was sitting outside our townhouse in Mountsorrel making the most horrendous noise.

I didn't need to open the curtains and peer out the window. The goose was well known to us by now, an unwelcome guest that had effectively moved in, patrolling the area outside our home like a security guard. All of which would have been fine but for the racket. Once it was in full voice, which was nearly always in the early hours, there was no stopping it.

If the goose was a pain in the arse for me, it was public enemy number one for Becky. She was heavily pregnant at the time and struggling to sleep well anyway, so the squawking and honking was the last thing she needed.

From canvassing locals to ringing the RSPCA, we tried everything but got absolutely nowhere, and we only became more frustrated as the bird kept coming back.

Desperate and deprived of sleep, we felt that we had little option but to take the goose on. I didn't fancy hand-to-hand combat, so I raided my fishing kit and went for the catapult. I'd come home from training on an afternoon, grab some small stones, take up my position on the top floor, load up the catapult and take aim. But all I'd achieve was to scare it off for a few hours.

It reached the stage where the goose became a topic of conversation wherever we went. One night, we were at a friend's house showing them the video we had of the goose on our phones, complete with the row it was making, and the couple were laughing about it. Then the bloke looked at me and said, 'Why don't you just shoot it?'

'What?' I replied, a bit taken aback. 'I haven't got a gun.'

'Borrow mine,' he said.

Becky and I both looked at each other. Had it really come to this? With bags under our eyes and our patience stretched to the limit, the answer could only be yes.

I'd loaded a gun before, but not since I was a kid, when a mate's dad had a rifle and we would go into their back garden and set up a target. Yet shooting a goose on the River Soar felt a bit different to getting closest to the bullseye. I'm an animal lover, so I knew that I had to go to war with my conscience before getting the goose in my sights.

Resisting the temptation to put a balaclava on, I went upstairs, opened the window, rested on the sill and waited. It was dark and I was sure that nobody could see me, neither the neighbours nor the goose, whenever it arrived. Everything was quiet outside and then, right on cue, it came into view. I looked through the scope on top of the rifle, wrapped my finger tightly around the trigger and did what I needed to do.

Bang! The goose was flapping like mad but, to my amazement, it stayed there, almost defiantly. I loaded the gun up again and fired a second shot, registering what I thought was another hit, and this time it staggered away, like a cat that wanders off to die.

The gun was returned – we couldn't wait to get it out of the house – and, finally, we had some peace and quiet. For about a day. The goose came back, noisier than ever, and I couldn't believe it. Neither could Becky.

'I thought you shot it,' she said.

'I did. I hit it twice,' I replied, feeling like I now had the goose and my fiancée against me, while also starting to wonder whether either pellet had struck the goose.

'Well, obviously you didn't hit it in the right spot,' Becky said. We were back to square one.

One day we went for a walk along the river and there it was, sitting on the bank, just staring back at us. There was a bloke on the boat that was moored up on the water next to it. Becky shouted over to him: 'Is that your goose?'

'Yeah,' he replied. 'Why, do you want to buy it?'

Becky's face was a picture. 'No, I want to effing kill it,' she said. 'That bloody goose sits outside my house every night and keeps me awake.' The guy didn't know what to say.

A little while later Becky went to a reflexology session, where she told the story of the now notorious goose. The therapist explained that geese are protective birds and highly sensitive, and suggested that it may have picked up on the fact that Becky was pregnant. It might have been trying to look after her and the baby.

With that, Becky went from being traumatised by the sound of the goose to feeling relief at hearing it, with the final twist being that as soon as Sofia, our daughter, was born and came home from hospital, the bird disappeared and was never seen again.

• • •

If all of that sounds slightly mad, it was totally in keeping with my first season as a Premier League footballer. I went from shooting a goose to eating an ostrich and, in a crazy game that thrust me into the spotlight in a way that I could never have imagined, marked my full Premier League debut with a goal and four assists in an improbable 5–3 victory over Manchester United at the King Power Stadium. What a day.

I missed the start of the season because I had a problem with my thigh, which I briefly forgot about during a rare night out at a friend's house. We were playing some drinking games and I decided to do a bit of breakdancing and perform the worm, which has always been a favourite of mine. Becky, who wasn't as impressed as everyone else, gave me a bollocking and reminded me that I was injured. Clearly that engagement ring I bought her at Tiffany's at Bangkok airport during preseason hadn't cut me as much slack as I'd thought.

Just after the opening day draw against Everton I signed a new contract, committing myself to Leicester for another four years, up until 2018, and taking my pay up to around £30,000 a week. I was now earning more in a week than I had in a year at Trulife, which is staggering when you stop to think about it, but I tried not to spend any time doing that. I left everything in my agent's hands and never made any demands to get me X, Y or Z because I trust John to get the best deal that he can for me. I do the football, he does the finances, and it's always been that way.

John did the negotiations with Terry Robinson, Leicester's director of football, and he insisted that the England clause stayed in. Terry, who I always got on well with, said that he 'didn't think I was an FA-type England player', so John called his bluff and suggested increasing the clause to £250,000. Terry didn't want to go down that path, so the figure stayed at £100,000. There was also a £6 million release clause inserted in the event of Leicester being relegated.

After missing the 2–0 defeat at Chelsea in the second match of the season, I got 20 minutes at home against Arsenal, and I came off the bench again a couple of weeks later when we won 1–0 at Stoke. The international break then gave me the chance to get up to speed for the visit of United, who'd spent around £150 million in the summer and were under new management following the appointment of Louis van Gaal.

It was a warm, sunny day in Leicester on 21 September 2014, and one of the things that sticks in my mind about that amazing afternoon, other than the extraordinary match, is the blessing I received before kick-off. Vichai, our owner, would regularly fly Buddhist monks from the Wat Traimit Withayaram Woraviharn (Golden Buddha) Temple in Bangkok to Leicester to give us spiritual support before a game, but they virtually gave me a shower that day.

We've all got individual pegs in the dressing room and the monks, dressed in saffron robes, go round each player in turn, dipping sticks in holy water and flicking them at you. But that day they came back a second time, tapped me on the head, said a prayer, and before I knew it I was getting smacked left, right and centre. I just had my tracksuit bottoms on at the time and I was absolutely drenched come the end.

Although some of the lads remove themselves from the equation because of their religion – Riyad, for example, is a Muslim, so he may feel that he doesn't want to be blessed by them, and everyone understands that – we all have the utmost respect for the monks. After all, it's part of Thai culture and the owner's religion, and we wouldn't be at the club if it wasn't for Vichai.

Whatever inspired us that day – whether it was the monks, the weather or the sight of a Man United team sheet that included Robin van Persie, Angel di Maria, Wayne Rooney and Radamel Falcao – it was an occasion that I will never forget. At the age of 27 I'd finally arrived. At least that's how it must have felt to those tuning in around the world to see a former factory worker with a mohawk – the haircut was back – wreaking havoc. It was the game of my life and the media had a field day.

Dave Kidd wrote in the *Daily Mirror*:

The contrast between Van Gaal's megastore till-ringers and Leicester match-winner Jamie Vardy is the stuff of comic-book absurdity. A Sheffield Wednesday reject and a former non-league journeyman signed from Fleetwood

Town, the 27-year-old Vardy stole the show on his first Premier League start against the most expensively assembled collection of forwards in English football history. Having once played for Stocksbridge Park Steels while wearing an electronic tag because of an assault conviction, Vardy is suddenly Roy Race with an ASBO.

United were 2–0 and then 3–1 up, and as the game started to turn, one of the abiding images for many people was the sight of Ryan Giggs, Van Gaal's assistant, hunched over in the dugout in a state of despair, with one hand covering his eyes. It was the first time in 853 Premier League matches that United had surrendered a two-goal lead and lost.

But what made me smile most was something that happened before the game rather than during it. In Van Gaal's pre-match press conference, someone asked him whether he knew much about Leicester and our attacking threats. With a pile of stuff stacked up next to him, he said, 'Of course. All these books are on Leicester and I've read every single one.' Obviously you didn't, Louis.

In fairness, everyone in a Leicester shirt was on top of their game against United, not just me. We were 2–0 down early on, but we never allowed our heads to drop and got a goal back straight from the restart, when Leonardo Ulloa headed home my cross. We fell 3–1 behind in the second half, but

Nuge scored a penalty after Rafael brought me down and then we had a touch of good fortune when Dean Hammond's shot, which was going miles wide, hit me. Luckily, I stopped it dead, and Esteban Cambiasso made it 3–3.

At that point we were absolutely pumped and sensed that United were there for the taking. Ritchie nicked the ball off Juan Mata and picked me out with a cross that I let hit me on the stomach, leaving me one-on-one with David de Gea. In our opposition analysis I'd watched clips of De Gea in one-on-one situations, and the United keeper doesn't really dive – he stands. It's like he tries to make the lower part of his body big by half-turning. So I just looked to slide the ball to his left … and I saw it roll into the net. *What a feeling*. Pumping my legs and arms like crazy, I ran towards the corner for the mother of all knee slides. I'd scored in the Premier League, against Manchester United, and we were 4–3 up. The ground was bouncing, literally – when you watch the footage back there's a Sky camera in the stand that's going up and down. Leo got the fifth, after Tyler Blackett was sent off for bringing me down, and it felt like a dream.

I was a pest all afternoon and that's what I've been wherever I've played, right back to those days at Colley Park with the Anvil. My finishing, the sort of composure I showed to beat De Gea that day, is something that I've worked on more and more the higher up I've gone. But the aggressive running, being a thorn in the opposition's side for 90 minutes, not giving them a moment's peace – that's always been there.

People were trotting out all sorts of statistics afterwards, going over my non-league days and mentioning that I'd joined a small group of players to score against both Manchester United and FC United, yet my mind was totally in the present. You never forget your roots – they made me what I am and I wouldn't change anything about my backstory – but once I got to the top flight I was thinking only about being a Premier League player. That meant trying to behave like one, too.

I was named the Barclays man of the match, did a live interview straight after the game and was back in front of the cameras again the following day, when we went to Leicester Racecourse and Sky Sports News wanted to do something with me. I was unrecognisable from the lad who would piss about and play the clown at Halifax. I'd turned into Serious Pete. That's not the real me that people see on TV. It's certainly not who I want to be, but it's who I have to be. I'd love to have a laugh, but it's just not appropriate when you're playing at the top level. I understand that because I'm not just representing myself, I'm also representing the club, so I have to say the right things. If I was 'the real Jamie Vardy' for a couple of minutes it would be carnage.

United felt like a watershed moment. By the end of the game I wasn't getting carried away, but I was thinking that

I'd made another step up and shown that I could handle the Premier League. We'd not only beaten one of the biggest clubs in the world, we'd put five past them after looking dead and buried. I sat there afterwards thinking, What could possibly go wrong now?

We lost eleven and drew two of the next thirteen matches, and I had to wait another six months before scoring again. After suffering a 2–1 defeat at home against Spurs on Boxing Day we were anchored to the bottom of the table, six points adrift of safety, and everybody was writing us off.

● ● ●

In the middle of all this Nigel got himself in a spot of bother when we lost 3–1 at home against Liverpool. He told a fan who was getting on the team's back to 'fuck off and die'. The first we knew about it was when we got in the players' lounge after the match and it was all over social media. Apparently, the person had been slating us, even though we were putting 100 per cent effort in, and Nigel snapped back.

It would be the first of three controversial incidents involving the manager that season. The second was during a 1–0 home defeat against Crystal Palace in February, when James McArthur slid off the pitch and accidentally knocked the gaffer over. We thought Nigel was messing about when he grabbed hold of McArthur, but he just didn't let him go of him.

The third flashpoint will always make me smile. We'd lost 3–1 at home against Chelsea, bringing to an end a four-game winning streak, and Nigel ended up calling a journalist an ostrich in his post-match press conference. I've watched the clip back so many times that I can recite what he said word for word: 'If you don't know the answer to that question, then I think you are an ostrich. Your head must be in the sand. Is your head in the sand? Are you flexible enough to get your head in the sand?'

I think it's hilarious, and I know all the lads thought the same as soon as we saw the footage. The following day at the training ground the chef captured the mood among the staff and players when he served ostrich burgers for lunch. Nigel had one of the burgers himself and had a laugh about it, and that's how he is, which probably jars with how he's perceived.

The Nigel Pearson portrayed by the media – dour and miserable and a bit confrontational – is not the Nigel that the players got to know. I actually think some of his behaviour in press conferences was his way of taking the heat off the lads, which we probably needed at times during that first season back in the Premier League.

The word 'bully' was bandied about after the ostrich episode. No chance. Maybe people thought he looked like one with his army haircut. I used to love giving him that one myself: 'Oh, you've had your hair cut, gaffer. From the marines?' He'd always have a chuckle.

Nigel's a straight talker, which is exactly what I am, so I got on great with him from day one. There's no bullshit. He tells it how it is, and if you do the business for him, he'll look after you. He's fiercely loyal and very protective of his players, not just by defending you against criticism, but by putting himself in the line of fire.

Don't get me wrong, I saw him lose his rag a few times, but it wasn't just for the sake of it. As long as you were giving Nigel everything, he was satisfied. Drop any hint that you weren't right at it and he was onto you, as I discovered one afternoon that season.

I trained badly one morning, which wasn't like me. We had the next day off, and Becky and I were off to Liverpool to see Gary Taylor-Fletcher, my old Leicester teammate, and his wife. We were already on the way when I got a message saying that the gaffer wanted to see me immediately, so we turned around and I went into the training ground wondering what it was about. 'Don't you start packing up on me now,' Nigel said to me in his office.

I told him I wasn't and that I'd just had an off day in training. I think the gaffer was worried that it was something deeper, but I promised him that wasn't the case. After everything he'd done for me, not just signing me from Fleetwood but standing by me in that difficult first season at Leicester, there was no way I was going to let him down. It was a good piece of management, really, because I think a chat like that gives you a gentle kick up the arse. I got back in the car even more determined to prove to him that I was bang at it.

Nigel remained positive throughout our bad run, perhaps mindful that showing any loss of belief would have transmitted to us. We just had to keep trying to turn the results around. It was strange because we weren't playing that badly – it wasn't as if we were ever getting battered, although in some ways that made it even tougher to accept. The only game I can remember being totally outplayed in was a 2–0 defeat at Southampton, when we set up with a diamond, as we did against United, and spent 90 minutes chasing shadows.

It was a big learning curve for us all, but with stability at home I was able to deal with the disappointment in a way that wouldn't have been possible a couple of years earlier. I was annoyed that I wasn't scoring, of course, and desperate to put that right, but this time I wasn't trying to find the answers at the bottom of a bottle of vodka or getting smashed with my mates to forget about it. I wanted to put it right on the training pitch, like everybody else.

There were occasions when I found myself in and out of the team, and also used in different positions. Sometimes I was wide on the right, with Nuge on the other flank and Leo, who'd joined from Brighton that summer, used through the middle. I played right-wing in the return match against Manchester United at Old Trafford, but for the majority of the first half I was more like a right-back. I always give everything wherever I'm asked to play, but that role just didn't suit me on the day and I got dragged off at half-time. At Arsenal in February we lost 2–1 – a fourth successive league defeat – and I didn't even make the bench. It was hard, not just for me, but for everyone at the club. I tried to keep everything in perspective, and changing nappies probably helped.

* * *

Sofia was born on 22 October 2014 and, in keeping with everything else that went on during the season, her birth wasn't straightforward. I dropped Becky off at hospital and went home to get the overnight bag, and while I was away the doctors discovered that the baby was not moving enough and her heartbeat was dropping. It looked like they were going to have to perform an emergency C-section, but her heart rate stabilised just as I returned, by which point Becky was behaving slightly oddly, deciding, for reasons only she can answer, to wash her hair.

Becky was put on a drip and wanted to be left alone, so I thought I should try to do something to occupy my time and give her some space. I turned on the iPad and found a

Champions League game to watch in the delivery room until the midwife told me that it was time. I gave Becky my titanium hand to squeeze – a special coil had been put in it after I lost that bout with the punching machine in Magaluf – and let her inflict all the pain she wanted as she gave birth to our first child together. We were both so happy.

Becky's children Megan and Taylor didn't live with us from the start. We knew that we weren't going to be in the rental property in Mountsorrel for long, so we didn't want the children to have to keep moving schools. As soon as we got the house in Melton Mowbray, a sleepy market town about half an hour from Leicester, Megan and Taylor moved in and we became a family unit. I said to the children at the outset that I wasn't there to replace anyone, but when Megan and Taylor are with me I treat them as if they are my own, and that's how I believe it should be.

In March we thought it would be a nice idea to have a housewarming and engagement party rolled into one, so we put up a huge marquee in the back garden that didn't go down too well with a few of the neighbours. We had about a dozen complaints before 10pm, and the police showed up a couple of days later to say that people had even been to the station to say how much they disapproved. It all seemed like a huge overreaction, maybe because Melton Mowbray was more used to hosting pie and cheese festivals. All I know is that we had a great time. We invited 80 guests, including all my teammates and their partners, and not only did everyone seem to enjoy themselves, I could see the togetherness among the lads that made me believe anything was still possible with our team.

There was only one player I wasn't sure about in our squad, and that was Esteban Cambiasso. He was signed on a free transfer from Inter Milan in the summer and was seen as a big coup for the club at the time. He'd played for Real Madrid, won La Liga, Serie A and the Champions League, and earned more than 50 caps for Argentina. But that meant fuck all to us as players. Many of us were now in our third season together and we were friends, not just teammates. It was always about the collective, right down to ensuring that when we organised the bonus system everyone in the match-day squad got the same amount whether they played for 90 minutes or didn't get off the bench. There was none of the pro-rata stuff you see at some other clubs. Everybody was treated the same.

Esteban was clearly a great player, and I don't think any of us had a problem with a big name coming in. But we didn't appreciate someone trying to take over, and that's how it felt at times with him. Wes was the skipper – and bloody brilliant at the job – but suddenly he was being undermined by someone who hadn't been at the club long. There were team meetings called just for the players, and you'd get there wondering what was going on only to find out that Esteban had organised it. You'd think, What's going on here?

We'd been conceding quite a few goals from set pieces during our poor run of results, so we were told to get our heads together the night before an away game and sort it out ourselves. We'd just finished dinner and Esteban stood up, picked up a pen and started to go through everything. I looked at him and thought, You're having a laugh. I don't think anyone was paying attention to anything he said.

What made things worse was that the lads started to feel that we were playing different formations just to fit him in. We were losing week in, week out, the team was getting chopped and changed – which is fair enough when the results are not good – but it seemed as though some of the boys were missing out so that Esteban could be accommodated.

Rumours started to circulate in the press that Esteban was on £20,000 a week more than the wage cap at the club. I never once heard anybody mention his salary in the dressing room – we didn't have players who were motivated by pound signs – but one day we were all talking away when Esteban stood up and said, 'I know that a lot of you probably think that I'm just here for the money, but I'm not.' It felt like a strange thing for him to come out with, because it wasn't as if anyone had said anything to Esteban, or anyone else, to prompt that remark.

At times it was like he was seeing things as if he was still playing for Real Madrid or Inter. He would spot a pass that his teammates at those top clubs would see and run on to, but as we'd not had that long to work with him – which was no fault of his own, to be fair – he'd play the pass and be disappointed that we'd not made the run.

I clashed with him towards the end of the season, when I had really bad bruising on the top of my foot, right under the laces where you strike the ball. It couldn't have been in a worse position, and the only way it would get better was through rest. When we played Tottenham away and lost 4–3 in March, I had a pain-killing injection in my foot, and I had to go through the same procedure before every game until the end of the season. It was just like a local anaesthetic, numbing the pain for two or three hours, and as soon as it wore off I was in agony again. Without it, I wouldn't have been able to play and I certainly couldn't train. Once I'd had my injection and played, my week was done.

I'd go out and watch when we were doing tactical work on the training ground, but other than that it was just a bike session in the gym. One day Esteban said to me, 'You never train, you.'

I was furious and replied, 'Why don't you shut up and put your staff shirt back on.' He didn't say anything back.

The defeat at Spurs had a silver lining, and not just because I scored for the first time since September. We played really well at White Hart Lane and I thought we deserved at least a point, so although the league table didn't make good reading – seven points adrift of safety with nine games remaining – we knew that if we carried on putting on that level of performance it was possible to stay up. At the same time it was going to need one hell of a run – a turnaround like the Premier League had never witnessed before.

Someone we signed in January convinced me that it could happen. Robert Huth, an experienced Premier League defender, joined on loan from Stoke and proved to be a brilliant addition both in the dressing room and on the pitch. He's such a funny lad, so dry with his humour, and he has this strange knack of rarely saying 'yes' to a question. Instead, he'll say something like, 'Does Rambo carry a knife?' There are a few centre-forwards who'd rather come up against Rambo than Huthy.

• • •

By the time West Ham visited the King Power Stadium on 4 April everybody knew that there was no margin for error. It was a must-win game if we were going to get out of the mess we were in. With four minutes to go and the score 1–1, the ball was cut back to me. I swung my left boot, hoping I'd get a good connection, mishit it, and luckily it went straight to Kingy, who couldn't have timed his 50th goal for the club any better. Finally, we had three points to show for our efforts, but we knew that we had to carry it on at West Brom the following week.

We were trailing 2–1 at half-time, and the gaffer changed things around, reverting to a 3-5-2 formation – a system that would go on to serve us well – and we dominated the second half. Huthy hauled us level, and in the second minute of injury time I robbed Gareth McAuley on the halfway line. He could have put it out for a throw-in or just hoofed it down the line, but instead he tried to drop his shoulder so he could pass back. I read his intentions, knocked him off the ball and I was away, with only Joleon Lescott to beat. I dragged the ball onto my left foot and drilled a low shot into the bottom corner.

One point had become three with almost the last kick of the game and I went ballistic. 'Who?' I said, jabbing a finger into my chest in front of our supporters, 'Fucking me!' I wasn't having a go at the fans – I was just showing how much it meant to me, especially after I'd not had the best of seasons. Truth be told, at times like that I'd like to be in with the supporters, jumping around without a care in the world. You could still hear them singing 'We are staying up' long after the final whistle.

Suddenly, there was a bit of momentum, and a week later it became three straight victories with a 2–0 win over Swansea, when Leo and Kingy did the business. We were now only in the relegation zone on goal difference. A huge win followed at Burnley, who were also fighting for their lives. Matty Taylor missed a penalty – I'd turned away and couldn't look when he started to run up – and 60 seconds later I was stabbing the ball over the line at the other end following a brilliant cross from Marc Albrighton. We were out of the bottom three.

Marc started coming into his own around that time, scoring the opening goal against Chelsea four days later, when he calmly slotted in my cut-back to give us the lead. He'd arrived from Villa on a free transfer in the summer and, to be honest, we couldn't believe they'd let him go. He's such a good team player. One of the lads was told that his nickname at Villa was 'Sharky', apparently because his nose looks like a shark fin, so that quickly caught on at Leicester.

We lost 3–1 against Chelsea, the champions elect, but played well. After the match I was walking through to the players' lounge when Jose Mourinho stopped me. He just looked at me and said, 'Do you ever stop fucking running?' I wasn't quite sure what to say at first, and eventually replied with a smile, 'No, that's what I'm out there to do.' As I walked off I thought, What a lovely compliment to receive from someone of Mourinho's standing.

While our defeat was overshadowed by talk of the ostrich, we knew we had to get straight back at it against Newcastle on the Saturday. We blew them away, going 3–0 up inside 48 minutes on a day when John Carver, the Newcastle manager, accused one of his own players of deliberately getting sent off with a challenge on me in injury time. Mike Williamson was the defender, and it was a good job that there was some padding around the TV camera on the side of the pitch, because I went flying into it after he caught me high and late. I ripped the skin off my hand, but it could have been a lot worse.

Carver was furious with Williamson. 'Vardy was five yards away, the ball as well. My initial reaction was, "Don't do it,"' the Newcastle manager said in the press conference afterwards. 'I'm not accepting that. I thought he meant it. I've said it to his face.'

I could see the tackle coming, but I couldn't get out of the way quickly enough. Only Williamson knows whether he nailed me to get sent off or not, but I'd never hang another player out to dry, so I dismissed Carver's comments when I was asked about them. I said that Williamson was probably guilty of a 'rush of blood to the head', no more than that.

We were still only one point above the relegation zone, despite winning five of our last six matches, so there was no room for complacency. But the mood among us was buoyant, and it didn't come as a surprise to anybody when we beat

Southampton 2–0 the following week. Riyad scored twice and showed exactly what he was capable of. I set up his second, which meant I'd assisted four and scored three in my last eight games, and there was some talk in the newspapers that Roy Hodgson, the England manager, had come along to see me play.

I took no notice of that whatsoever. I was far more interested in hearing the news on Matty James, who was taken off on a stretcher with what looked like a serious injury. The following week it was confirmed that he'd suffered a rupture of the anterior cruciate ligament. I was absolutely gutted for him, not only as a mate, but also because he'd been so important to us that season.

With only two fixtures to go, there was daylight – three points – between us and the relegation zone. Our fate was firmly in our own hands. We went to Sunderland, who were only a point behind us, and I don't think I've ever done so much running in a game. It finished 0–0, and at the full-time whistle I was lying on the pitch, staring up at the sky with absolutely nothing left in the tank. When I got to my feet I could see all the lads jumping around and hugging one another. We'd done it! We'd pulled off the Great Escape. What a feeling – we were going to get another shot at the Premier League.

9

'PLAYERS NEED TO BRING THEIR PASSPORT BUT WILL NOT REQUIRE AN ENGLAND SUIT'

The text message seemed to go on for ever. I didn't have the name of the person who sent it in my phone, and my first reaction was that somebody was taking the piss. I was out shopping for holiday clothes with Becky in Leicester at the time, three days before the end of the season, and my mind was wandering towards the beach and a much-needed rest with my family. Then my phone beeped. I read the first line and I was frozen to the spot. The rest of the message was more like an essay and I started to wonder if it was ever going to come to an end.

It was sent on 21 May 2015, at 12:05pm, and read:

This is to confirm that you have been selected in the England senior squad for the games versus Republic of Ireland on Sunday 7 June in Dublin and Slovenia on Sunday 14 June in Ljubljana. The squad will meet up at St George's Park on Wednesday 3 June at 12:30 for lunch. The team will be flying out to Dublin on the Saturday before the match on the Sunday. After the Republic of Ireland game you will be able to return home. The squad will meet up at the Grove on Wednesday 10 June at 12:30 in preparation for the game against Slovenia. The team will fly out on the Saturday ahead of the game on Sunday. We return home immediately after the game. Players need to bring their passport but will not require an England suit. You will need to bring boots (two pairs of each type of match boots, i.e. studs and moulds), shin pads and trainers. Please report in your Nike tracksuit, with maroon top and navy bottoms and maroon Nike polo shirt from the previous get together if you have one, and bring with you your Nike luggage if this has previously been issued to you. Please let us know as soon as you can if you will need a car to pick you up on Wednesday morning. Seni or I will be in touch with regard to your transport arrangements.

I passed the phone to Becky for her to have a read, and we both looked at each other afterwards and didn't know what to say. I decided to ring Dave Rennie, the physio at Leicester, because I knew that the England doctors and medical staff had been in touch with him asking about players, to check on injuries and fitness.

'Someone is pulling my pants down here, Dave. Someone is taking the piss,' I said.

'No, you're in,' Dave replied, with a little laugh. 'Congratulations.'

And there it was, ten minutes later, flashing up on websites everywhere and rolling along the bottom of the screen on Sky Sports News, confirming that Roy Hodgson had named three new faces – me, the Queens Park Rangers striker Charlie Austin and Burnley goalkeeper Tom Heaton – in his 24-man squad for the friendly against the Republic of Ireland and the Euro 2016 qualifier against Slovenia.

My phone went into meltdown. Occasionally, I'd glance back to that original text message, read through it again and try to make sense of it. 'What the fuck is going on?' was the only thing I could think.

I didn't respond to the text, which was from Michelle Farrer, England's director of team operations. I didn't know if I was supposed to reply for a start. I'd never been in this position before, obviously, and there was far too much to take in anyway.

When my mobile died it felt like a blessing, and I made a conscious decision not to charge it up again until I went to bed because I wanted to let everything sink in. Jamie Vardy, playing for England? I couldn't get my head around it. Two years earlier I'd wanted to go back to Fleetwood.

Perhaps Michelle picked up on the radio silence, because I got another text from her the following day, at 9:15pm, saying that she would 'catch up with me next week to chat through arrangements, and meeting up with England, nothing to worry about, all straightforward'. So I replied, saying, 'OK, thank you.' That was it. Three words in response to about three hundred.

There'd been a bit of speculation in the days leading up to the announcement, but I didn't believe what I'd read, and it wasn't as if anybody at the FA had got in touch with me to give me the nod that something could happen. So I was just a bit blown away by it all.

On the day of the squad announcement Roy gave a press conference and talked about how he'd gone to see me in that game at Kidderminster, three years earlier in March 2012, when he was in charge of West Brom and I was playing for Fleetwood – thankfully, he didn't mention the lunge near the touchline. 'He was getting a lot of good reviews and we thought it was an ideal opportunity to watch him play,' Roy said. 'It was a cold night, a difficult surface, and, to be honest, he didn't get a lot of chances to show what he could do. But you could see then he had some ability.

'Myself, Ray Lewington and Gary Neville have followed him. His latter part of the season at Leicester, through their Great Escape, has been really excellent. He has some interesting qualities and this will be a chance to see them at close hand.'

At the time, England were without Daniel Sturridge through injury, Danny Welbeck had some fitness issues and Rickie Lambert was short of match practice. Harry Kane, Danny Ings and Saido Berahino had been called up for the European Under-21 Championship, so Hodgson's decision to name me and Charlie in the squad was seen by many as a reflection of England's lack of options up front, rather than anything we'd done to merit being included, and it was pretty clear that quite a few of the newspapers didn't think I'd ever be in this situation again.

'While the fairytale rise of Vardy is a cause for celebration for him, it asks wider questions again about the quality of English players at Hodgson's disposal,' wrote the *Independent*, before reeling off the names of Michael Ricketts, Franny Jeffers, Nuge, Dean Ashton, Kevin Davies, Jay Bothroyd and Fraizer Campbell. All of them played once for England and never again.

The *Daily Mirror* flagged up how I'd been booked more times (six) than I'd scored goals (four) for Leicester that season, and in *The Times* they wrote about 'an appealing story, albeit one that is unlikely to signal the start of a long international career'.

All of which I could understand, to an extent. To be honest, I thought I'd only been called up because people like Kane and Berahino had gone with the Under-21s, and I was effectively just making the numbers up. Yet nobody at Leicester was going to rain on my parade. We were off on the day that the England squad was named, so when I drove in to training on the Friday I could see *Leicester Mercury* billboards – there's a newsagent's on the corner of Banks Road, where you turn off Aylestone Road to pass through the residential streets that lead to the training ground – with the words 'England call-up for City striker' splashed across them. It was real.

When I got to the training ground the lads were thrilled for me, shaking my hand and congratulating me – as well as indulging in a bit of standard piss-taking. The gaffer was also delighted and said as much in his press conference that morning, when he may have had Skittle vodka and a few other misdemeanours in mind as he touched on the problems I'd overcome. 'It's quite an amazing turnaround,' Nigel said. 'When you look at his career in its entirety, it's a good story. It's probably the type of story that hasn't happened in recent generations of players.

'Jamie's not as straightforward a character as you would probably think he is, for lots of different reasons, and they're not for discussion here. He's had a few situations that he's had to deal with on and off the field. And, as most players do from time to time, he's suffered with confidence, which had coincided with other aspects he's had to deal with. But he's a likeable lad. He's someone I have an awful lot of time for. I'm really pleased for him. I hope he's able to enjoy the experience.'

I was excited, of course – it's the absolute pinnacle to be asked to represent your country, especially when you've been on my journey – but I also felt that our plans for the summer had just been thrown up in the air. As soon as the season was over, against QPR on the Sunday, we were due to go away. It was also Becky's sister's wedding the night before the Republic of Ireland game, and we'd booked to go to the Turks and Caicos Islands, in the Caribbean, two days later.

I started thinking about it more and more and, as crazy as it sounds, I got it into my head that I wasn't going to join up with the England squad. I went to see Dave Rennie and said, 'Can you not tell them I'm injured?'

I told Nigel I wasn't going – and a part of me was serious when I said it. The season was just about to finish and, as a professional footballer, as soon as it's over that is your one chance all year to have a proper break, escape with the family and relax. We have plenty of afternoons off at home, of course, and as someone who spent four-and-a-half years doing shift work in a factory I appreciate the free time you get as a professional footballer as much as anyone. But a holiday is different, and I was ready for one come the end of that season. I felt mentally and physically exhausted.

Some people at the club probably wondered if I was making an excuse. They may have thought that I was daunted by the prospect of going away with England and stepping out of my comfort zone, almost as if it was all a bit too much for me. But none of that was true.

I'm not going to lie – there were some nerves. But the main thing – and I don't want people to interpret this the wrong way – was the inconvenience. We had so much on that summer, and for ages I'd been looking forward to switching off and relaxing. We'd planned to go away with our children and two other families, Gary Taylor-Fletcher's and Ritchie de Laet's, to have this unbelievable holiday together, plus the wedding. All of a sudden, it was gone.

The gaffer soon picked up on the fact that it wasn't just a throwaway comment when I said I wasn't going. He dragged me into the office at the training ground and said, 'You're going. Stop being an idiot. Just go and show them what you can do.'

Looking back now, I think it just hadn't sunk in and I couldn't deal with a dramatic change to my life. In the end, I knew that I couldn't turn down the chance to represent my country, and I didn't want to, either. What I didn't realise was just how much I'd enjoy it with England, because by the time I returned from Slovenia I was praying that I'd get another chance.

• • •

St George's Park, the national football centre in Burton upon Trent, is a vast place and hugely impressive. I accepted the FA's offer to send someone to drive me there, and the journey, which was just over an hour's drive from my house in Melton Mowbray, gave me the chance to sit back and think about everything. It still felt very surreal.

I'd spent nine years in non-league football and been an England fan for a long time, never with any thoughts whatsoever about playing for the national team. Why would you when you're working in a factory at the age of 24?

If England were playing on TV and I didn't have a game, I'd be watching. Sometimes that would be at home, but more often than not I'd be in a pub with my mates – usually the Old Blue Ball in Hillsborough. I'd go through the same emotions as England fans all over the country, with the only difference being that some people probably controlled theirs better than me.

I was in the Old Blue Ball when England lost against Germany in the 2010 World Cup in South Africa, when Frank Lampard's shot crossed the goal line by about a yard but the referee didn't give it. Everyone was absolutely raging in the pub, going mental with the referee for not seeing it, and I ended up throwing my pint at the big screen as my frustration got the better of me. Not one of my finer moments, admittedly, but that's how much I got wrapped up in England matches.

A few of the lads who were there that day would have been at the greyhound evening in Sheffield shortly after I signed for Leicester, when we had the England–San Marino game on in our hospitality box. It's safe to say that it wouldn't have entered anyone's head that less than three years later I'd be joining up with a lot of those England players.

So, all in all, there was quite a bit to digest on the way to St George's Park and, while I'm not someone who generally lets anything bother them, it was actually quite nerve-wracking that first day. While I knew all the players – not personally, but obviously I recognised everyone – it was different with some of the staff, and as I was getting introduced to them I started worrying about how I would remember their names.

There were two things that helped me feel at ease. The first was that all the England lads were brilliant and made sure that I felt welcome. The second was that Charlie Austin was in exactly the same position as me, not only in terms of it being his first call-up, but also because he had a backstory similar to my own. Charlie was working on a building site and playing for Poole Town in the Wessex League Premier Division at the same time as I was turning out for Stocksbridge Park Steels. We'd both come from non-league football and could relate to how the other was feeling about being in that England environment.

In many ways it was like the first day at a new school. I remember filling my plate with food, going to the dinner table and, as the new lad, not being quite sure where to sit. In the end I just thought, Sod it, and parked my arse on a table with James Milner, Phil Jagielka, Joe Hart, Wayne Rooney, Gary Cahill and Tom Heaton.

Obviously, you've got no idea what to expect in that sort of situation. At club level you hear that certain teams have someone with a bit of an ego, but there was none of that in the England squad. The banter on the table while we were eating was unbelievable, everyone having a laugh and a joke, and that was something that took me by surprise. I'd thought it would be really formal.

Some of the lads are so different from the public perception, and no one more so than Milner. Without a doubt, 'Milly' is one of the funniest guys I've ever met. This is the same person who's got a fake Twitter account called Boring James Milner. Let me set the record straight: he's nothing like the way he's portrayed, and Danny Drinkwater would back me up on this. When Drinky was called up the following year he sat at the same table as Milly and was in stitches every time we had a meal.

Milly has as good a laugh at the Boring James Milner page as anyone, and we'd often all be pissing ourselves looking at it. That's what it was like during those early call ups – totally relaxed.

Away from the dinner table I had to be Serious Pete again, because within 24 hours of arriving at St George's Park I was asked to sit down in front of the media. I think sometimes a few of the senior lads try to make sure that you don't do any press or broadcast interviews when it's your first call-up because it's daunting enough coming into the squad anyway. But the FA decided that, as Charlie and I were in the same boat, they'd make us available.

It was totally different to anything I'd ever faced before. I'd done quite a few one-on-one interviews with national newspaper journalists and post-match stuff with Sky, when you know millions of people are watching, but with England there were so many more reporters in the room, and it's quite a lot to deal with the first time. I had to do separate media conferences for press, radio and TV, all the while sitting there with an England tracksuit on. It still felt a bit strange when I caught sight of my reflection.

One of the reporters asked me if that famous United game back in September was the making of me, and I replied, 'Yeah. But then I went missing for six months.'

There was another question I knew would come up, even though I'd addressed it plenty of times before. It was inevitable that someone would ask me about the assault conviction and the electronic tag. I don't like that but I understand it – I did what I did and I have to live with the consequences, which is why I'll never sidestep it whenever the question is asked.

From my point of view there's nothing to hide. I've got a criminal record. I'm not proud of it or how I behaved that night outside the Leadmill, but I'm not ashamed of what I did either, because of the story behind that incident. The explanation I gave at St George's Park was nothing that I hadn't said before, but once I'd been asked, I thought I should let every journalist in there know. And, of course, I knew that it was going to generate more headlines than it ever had before because I was speaking as an England player.

Away from the cameras and microphones, Roy and Ray Lewington, the assistant manager, went out of their way to have a personal chat with me to help me feel more comfortable. They both told me how impressed they were with how I'd played for Leicester during the run-in, and they made a special point of saying how much they liked what I did when we didn't have the ball. I'm a grafter and I make sure that, one way or another, I get the ball back as high up the pitch as possible. They thought that it could maybe help England, which was nice to hear, and it gave me a bit of encouragement on the eve of the Ireland game.

Becky and I had managed to get our holiday moved and, thanks to FaceTime, I was in a hotel in Dublin at the same time as the wedding in Oxfordshire. I got passed round to just about everyone at Heythrop Park that afternoon, from Becky and the kids to the bride and groom, so in the end I was there, in a manner of speaking, even if the suit I'd bought never got worn. Not that I was worried about that any more. The England jersey felt a lot better. What an unbelievable feeling to pull on the shirt with the three lions on it.

Nuge texted me before the game, saying: 'Go out and do what we all know you can'. Then he sent another text straight afterwards, saying: 'One game, one goal!' A reminder about the moment he came on for England against Andorra, in 2007, and scored in the last minute. No pressure, in other words.

Roy named the team and I was on the bench, as expected. I just hoped that I would get a chance to come on, no matter how late in the game. I'd been through my usual pre-match routine to make sure that I felt as comfortable as possible. The England staff asked me on day one what I did before Leicester matches to prepare, so I told them. There was no point lying, and it's not as if I was going to be able to sneak a load of Red Bull cans into the hotel or my kitbag.

In truth, it wasn't much of a match in Dublin. There was little in the way of goalmouth action and it was difficult to see anybody scoring, but I wasn't bothered by any of that –

I just wanted to be out there. Not long before the hour mark Roy told me and Phil Jagielka to go and warm up because we were both going on after his first two substitutions. My first thought was, Fuck!

Ross Barkley and Andros Townsend were brought on not long afterwards, so I set off to do a few more stretches with a touch under 20 minutes to go, and then I got the shout to get ready. Roy made me feel relaxed by just asking me to do exactly what had earned me the call-up in the first place. I got stripped, Dave Watson, the England goalkeeping coach, went through the set-piece routines, and I stood on the edge of the pitch, in front of about 40,000 Irish fans, waiting for a stoppage in play.

I knew that I was going on to play down the middle, but I didn't have a clue who I was coming on for. Then the board came up and it was Wayne Rooney, of all people. Wazza said, 'All the best,' to me as he came off and that was it. There I was, number 19, running out onto the pitch with an England shirt on.

'And here, at the age of 28, comes cap number one for Jamie Vardy,' said Clive Tyldesley, commentating for ITV. 'What a story this is. Released by Sheffield Wednesday as a teenager, he was celebrating a Conference title victory with Fleetwood three years ago. Five years ago he was making medical splints for a living. His first season at Leicester wasn't up to much. Boy, how he has blossomed since.'

I went down in the record books as the seventeenth Leicester player to represent England and the first since Ian Walker, in 2004. I didn't have any chances – there weren't many in the game full stop – but I loved every minute and, as ever, just tried to be a nuisance. I doubt anybody will remember that Ireland game with much fondness, but for me it was everything. I was in absolute dreamland.

Gareth Seddon, my old Fleetwood teammate, said beforehand that there wouldn't be anyone prouder than me to wear an England shirt, and he was absolutely spot on. Everyone signed it for me afterwards, and when I got back home I had it framed.

John, my agent, was away on a family holiday in Majorca at the time, gutted to miss out on seeing me make my England debut. One of the other agents at Key Sports sent John a picture message not only of me coming on, but also the clock in the top left-hand corner of the TV screen, which was stopped at 74:03. That time had special significance – not that I was aware of it as I stood there, dry-mouthed, waiting to get on the pitch.

John's persistence in getting that England clause inserted finally looked like it had paid off. My contract said that I was entitled to a one-off £100,000 payment if I started for my country or came on before the 75th minute. That sort of wording is fairly commonplace because clubs want to protect themselves from paying out appearance money for someone who makes it onto the pitch for only a few minutes and doesn't contribute anything to the game.

It later became a slight issue with Leicester because there was a bit of a dispute as to whether the clause had been triggered or not. The substitution was in the 75th minute of the game but, to be exact, it was 74 minutes and 3 seconds on the clock.

My agent ended up sending me the same photograph that he'd received, which I then showed to a few people at the club, and after some toing and froing it got sorted when Jon Rudkin, the director of football, and the owners got involved. That England shirt, however, meant far more to me than any sum of money.

Nobody criticised me for how I played against Ireland. I think everybody recognised that it was a difficult game to make much of an impression. But in the match reports the following day the vibe was pretty much the same as it had been when news first broke that I'd been called up. 'Jamie Vardy replaced Rooney as a second-half sub, and while his fairytale climb from non-league to full international is a terrific story, it will surely be a short-lived one,' was one of the lines in the *Sun*.

Yet my thought process had changed a little by now. While I'd initially understood the one-cap wonder talk and in some ways subscribed to that view myself, after I came on against

Ireland I saw things a bit differently. If I was just making the numbers up, then what was the point of Roy bringing me on?

A week later I was among the substitutes in Slovenia but didn't get on – in a game where Jack Wilshere scored two superb goals and Wazza got a late winner to give us a 3–2 victory – and that was me done. After all the fuss at the beginning, I left the England camp desperately hoping I'd be invited back. Once you've had that chance and been involved, training for a week or two with the country's best players, you don't want to let it go.

* * *

I had a few weeks to switch off before reporting back with Leicester for the new season, so Becky and I went away to Ibiza – the quiet(ish) side of the island – where Becky somehow broke her toe wrestling but still managed to wear a pair of heels to the nightclub Pacha for a hippy-themed party, and then we headed off to Turks and Caicos, a little later than planned, with the children.

Straight away, I could tell that something was different. It just felt like my profile had gone to another level. Loads of people were asking for a photo, which hadn't really happened that much outside of Leicester before. I'd happily stand and smile, although the only exception to that rule was when I had Sofia in my arms. I didn't want to be photographed then. Most people were respectful, but some blokes would get annoyed or offended. 'Well, give her to your missus,' one guy said.

Another by-product of fame involved people trawling through social media to see what I'd posted in the past. They dug up a few pearlers, chief among them the four words that appeared on my Facebook account the night after Fleetwood won 4–2 at Stockport, when I was suspended and Peter Crouch was in the crowd. 'Chat shit, get banged' became the stock response to anything I tweeted around the time of the Great Escape and my England debut. People would shout it across the street to me. I started to see T-shirts with it on and, incredibly, tattoos of it.

I became more and more intrigued, because I couldn't remember what the story was behind me updating my Facebook status with those words, although it clearly happened – there were the screenshots to prove it. The chances are that someone has chatted shit and got banged over the years, but the honest truth is that I don't know what prompted me to write that in Blackpool at 10:45pm on 28 September 2011. I thought it might be a line I'd taken from a film, but that doesn't seem to be the case. I've wracked my brain, looked back to try to get some context and searched the internet for ages, but the only thing that comes up in association with those words is my name. What on earth had I started?

Back in Turks and Caicos, I was enjoying some welcome chill-out time and a rum punch when I received some text messages from a few of my mates, saying 'something must have happened at Leicester because Pearson is odds-on to be sacked'. Obviously, I was aware of the Thailand episode at the end of the season, which led to three young players having their contracts terminated, including Nigel's son, after their involvement in a sex tape. I didn't go on that tour and, as more than a month had passed since, I didn't think the incident would lead to Nigel going. Yet within an hour of the lads getting in touch with me, the news that Nigel had departed was everywhere. We never heard exactly what happened. All that was said was that it was the right decision from the club's point of view. You just have to respect that and get on with it. That's the nature of football. But it doesn't mean that you forget what someone did for you.

After plenty of speculation about who would take over, it was announced on 13 July that Claudio Ranieri would be our new manager. I remembered him from his time at Chelsea, when he was known as the Tinkerman, and knew he'd managed some big clubs since, but I don't think any of us were really sure what to expect, as is often the case with a new gaffer.

We'd already reported back for preseason by the time Claudio was appointed, so Walshy and Shakey took training in Austria initially. Claudio arrived a couple of days later and got us together for a meeting, where he made it clear that he didn't think anything major needed to be done to the squad.

'I watched all your run-in from the end of last season and I love what I see,' he told us. 'I love the way you fight for each other and that's what I want from you. I don't want to make any big changes. I might just tweak little things.'

Claudio went on to say that he wouldn't be taking any training sessions that week. He would leave the existing staff to take care of things while he looked on from the side, where he could run the rule over everyone.

We were relieved to hear that Claudio wouldn't be tearing things up, because we didn't feel that much needed altering. It was only six weeks earlier that we'd pulled off the Great Escape, winning seven out of our last nine league matches, so there was plenty to build on.

The team spirit was as strong as ever, and I was up to my usual antics, with Ritchie de Laet my partner in crime in Austria. With everyone asleep, we decided to creep into the kit room, where we found Kasper Schmeichel's gear neatly laid out. Our eyes lit up, because we knew that Kasper, who's Mr Serious, very professional and likes everything to be done just right, wouldn't be happy if we did anything. So we opened the windows on the top floor and launched everything out.

The next morning, he came for me straight away.

'All my kit, my boots, everything – some of it is on the roof, some is at the front of the hotel,' he said.

'I don't know what you're talking about,' I said, with the straightest face ever.

'I know it's you,' he replied, clearly annoyed.

'Kasper, I don't know what you're on about,' I said.

Kasper kept going on and wouldn't let it lie. He was pissed off, but I denied all knowledge and knew that he didn't have any evidence, other than the fact that I tended to be behind most of the practical jokes at the club. However, it soon became clear that there was another prankster in town that summer.

Christian Fuchs, an experienced Austria international, joined on a free transfer from Schalke and would go on to become a terrific character in the dressing room as well as an excellent left-back. I got roped into his #NoFuchsGiven video challenges when we played Egg Russian Roulette at the training ground one morning. There were half-a-dozen eggs in a tray, half of them hard-boiled, and you had to crack them on each other's heads, hoping you'd pick the right ones.

As well as the arrival of Christian, Shinji Okazaki signed from Mainz and Huthy turned his loan from Stoke into a permanent deal, which meant that there was a little bit of singing to do while we were away in Austria, as part of the new players' initiation ceremony.

I've sang for the lads loads of times. Any night we've had a karaoke evening, Kasper and I take over and sing a few boyband classics – I love a bit of Westlife. But the new boys had to do it during dinner, so a chair was pulled to the side for them to stand on.

Shinji was absolutely brilliant. He did a Japanese pop song and none of us knew what he was saying, but he was body-bopping to it superbly so we all joined in with him. Huthy did a song from DJ Otzi, which meant nothing to me until he started and I realised it was 'Hey Baby (Uhh, Ahh)'. As for Christian, let's just say that the lads weren't happy. He said he was dedicating it to his little boy … and then did 'Twinkle, Twinkle, Little Star'. A bloody nursery rhyme.

We returned from Austria to play our first preseason friendly under Claudio on the same day that Esteban Cambiasso announced he was leaving the club. Some of Esteban's goals were crucial in the Great Escape season, like the one against West Ham at home near the end, but none of us were bothered when we heard the news. People see what they want to see when they judge players, but if Esteban was that influential at Leicester he'd have won the players' player of the year award.

Football moves on. Esteban left, and two weeks later we signed a guy called N'Golo Kanté. Job done.

10

IN THE EYE OF A STORM

Most convictions get wiped after a period of time. But there's no way of erasing what happened at a casino in Leicester in the early hours of the morning in July 2015. The word 'racist' is a permanent stain against my name. It's worse than a criminal record.

I've done everything I can to try to repair the damage, most importantly of all to the person I racially abused, who thankfully accepted my apology. Some people, I know, will never forgive me. Others will accept that I made a terrible mistake and recognise that I have learnt from it. But whatever anyone thinks, good or bad, there are constant reminders of the incident that I have to live with and, more distressingly from my point of view, so do my children.

It's there on YouTube when they type in their dad's name and it comes up 'Jamie Vardy racist'. On Google, too. It's horrible. It's not tomorrow's fish-and-chip paper – it's never going away.

For some, it colours their perception of me, even though we've never exchanged a word. These people don't know me. They've watched some footage or read an article and made a judgement: Jamie Vardy's a racist.

But that is not me in any way. I cannot stress this enough.

I like a drink and enjoy being Jack the Lad. I've worked in a pub and played for one, had a few scraps and spent a night in a police cell. I can be loud and a pain in the arse at times. But one thing I'm not, and never will be, is a racist. I looked in the eyes of the student I verbally abused and told him that. I needed him to see, not just hear via a statement, how sorry I was for the way I behaved towards him. I wanted him to know that there was ignorance, not malice or prejudice, behind the word I used at the casino.

I was angry at the time and I'd had too much to drink – they're facts, not things I'm trying to use in my defence – but I'd never have used the word 'Jap' if I'd known it was racist. And because I'm now aware of the exact meaning behind it, and how derogatory and disparaging a term it is, the footage gets worse every time I look at it.

I'm definitely not looking for – or expecting – any sympathy, and I know that I'm not the victim here. I'm just trying to explain how I feel and stress that I do care about what happened. I'm a father and a husband, a footballer in a multicultural dressing room, and 'racist' is the last word that I want to be associated with.

So many times I've wished that we'd never gone out that night. Or that we'd decided to go somewhere else. Most of all, I wish that it had never happened. But it did, and I have to live with that.

• • •

Retracing the steps of what went on that evening begins with a preseason friendly at Mansfield Town on Saturday 25 July 2015, two weeks before the opening day of the Premier League season and not long after we'd returned from our training camp in Austria. We drew 1–1, and later in the day Becky and I arranged to go out for some food at TGI Friday's in Leicester with Nuge and his partner, Chloe.

We'd had a few drinks, and we were thinking about whether to go to a nightclub or the casino, where we knew a couple of the other lads were likely to be. In the end we decided against the nightclub. I've always liked a trip to the casino – I enjoy a gamble now and again, just for a bit of fun – but what I like more is the fact that it's a place where I can have a drink, play a bit of cards and, because of the rules inside a casino, there won't be someone coming up to me with a mobile phone every ten seconds to take a picture. There's a time and a place for that, of course, but we certainly didn't fancy it that night.

We got to Grosvenor Casino, on Highcross Street in Leicester, somewhere between 10:30 and 11pm. To begin with we were playing roulette, and then I asked for a poker table to be opened, which the casino agreed to do in an area just off the main floor. Andrej Kramarić, our Croatian winger, was also in there that evening, playing in a poker tournament.

Ritchie de Laet arrived not long afterwards with his tennis coach, and they joined our table, where Nuge and I were playing. Becky was sitting alongside me, and I think Chloe had gone off to play on the slot machines for a bit. We were playing a cash game of poker, so you play with chips, there's no set period of time for how long it goes on and players can get up and go as and when they want.

Other than our group, there were four other players at the table, plus the dealer. We'd been playing for a while and everything was fine. There was quite a bit of money in the pot – a couple of thousand pounds – and because so many players were involved, everyone was holding their cards close, being careful not to show their hand.

An Asian lad then walked all the way around the table and went back to talk to one of the players in the game sitting on the opposite side to us. I wasn't comfortable with what he was doing, so I said, 'Why are you looking at our cards?' He denied he was, but then the player he'd spoken to said, 'All in'.

Fuck that. 'No chance,' I said. 'You've just seen my cards.'

The dealer got involved and said, 'What's the issue?'

The guy opposite then made me even more angry by saying, 'He has seen your cards, but he's not told me anything.'

I thought they were taking the piss out of me. I was furious. In my eyes I was being turned over, so I threw my cards in and accused him of cheating.

I asked the dealer to get the casino manager, and the Asian lad walked away from our table and over to where the poker tournament was taking place nearby. I stood up and, with frustration building inside of me, said, 'Yo, Jap. Walk on.'

I said it three times. I wanted his attention because I was pissed off with him.

He came back, so we were only a few yards away from one another, and apologised for any offence he may have caused by looking at my cards. He went on to say that he always did it and nobody had ever said anything before, and then he walked off.

At that point I started getting text messages from a friend saying that someone was making comments about my behaviour on Twitter and had taken a photo of me at the poker table and copied in a newspaper and TV station. My friend had given me the name of the person who'd tweeted, so I shouted out his name and he turned around. I had a go at him for taking pictures and posting them, and we ended up arguing.

Then a middle-aged guy came in from the smoking area, not far away from our table, and had a pop at me. I can't remember the exact words, but it was something along the lines of, 'Because you play for Leicester, you think you're it. You come in here, acting big time.'

And that's when I saw red. The bloke was nothing to do with what was happening, and as far as I was concerned he hadn't seen everything that had gone on. It had all become too much. I got off my chair, knocking the drinks over in the process, and started swearing aggressively. Becky had hold of my wrist and Ritchie came over to restrain me.

I'm not going to try and defend any of it, but the way the clip was edited on the newspaper's website made it look like I was effing and blinding at the young Asian lad, when that wasn't the case. Of course, that doesn't make it right that someone else was the subject of my anger, but at that moment in time I just couldn't handle another person getting involved.

Becky told Ritchie to take me to the toilets upstairs to chill out. On the way there, the middle-aged man was standing with his back to the bar, smirking at me, so I made another comment. Something else I shouldn't have done, but by that point my head had gone. Becky called security over, and the casino manager dealt with the lad who was taking pictures. He was escorted out and made to delete what was on his phone, because you're not allowed to take photos in there.

We left not long afterwards, back to Melton Mowbray in a taxi, and the journey home could not go quickly enough. I just wanted to wake up in my bed and think that none of it had really happened, that it was all a bad dream – and that was before I realised the true gravity of what I'd just done.

Before we pulled up at our house, Becky predicted that it wouldn't be the last we'd hear of the incident. Yet nobody mentioned the word 'racism'. Not around the poker table. Not in the casino, where Nuge and Ritchie carried on playing with the same people after we left. And not in the cab on the way home. I knew my behaviour was unacceptable and that the red mist had descended in a way that hadn't happened for years. But I didn't know that I was guilty of racially abusing anybody.

We heard nothing for several days, leaving me to mull over the scene in the casino and try to work out why it had blown up in the way that it did. It was too easy to blame alcohol – I've had something to drink hundreds of times and not lost control in that way. I didn't have the answers, but I knew that it could never happen again.

The silence was broken on Friday 31 July, when the *Sun* newspaper got in touch with Leicester. They alleged that I'd racially abused someone in the casino and said that they had footage.

Jon Sanders, Leicester's player liaison officer, called me. He was with Claudio and Jon Rudkin, the director of football. They put me on loudspeaker and asked me what had happened. The newspaper had let them know the term I used, and I told them exactly what I'm writing here now – I didn't realise that it was offensive, let alone racist. I thought it was like calling someone a Brit or an Aussie, and only now do I realise how ignorant that was on my part.

By the time we'd finished talking, the full implications were starting to become clear. I felt numb. I wanted to speak to the young lad I'd abused and apologise to him. I was sick with worry as I thought about what this all meant for my career and my family. Suddenly, I could see everything that I'd worked for unravelling in front of my eyes.

Leicester made contact with the casino. Anthony, the club's head of media, also spoke to the press office at De Montfort University after establishing that two of those involved – the lad I'd offended and the guy who was tweeting from the casino – were students there. And, of course, there was dialogue with the *Sun*, who had the story but seemed to be sitting on it.

We played against Sunderland on 8 August, the opening day of the season, and won 4–2. I scored the first goal, but those close to me already knew that my 11th minute header wouldn't be making the headlines the following day. Becky received a call from my agent on Saturday morning, after I'd already left, to say that the casino incident was going to be on the front page the next morning, together with video footage online. She said nothing to me before the match because she didn't want it to affect how I played, but as soon as the game was over she broke the news. I was full of dread.

We returned home from the King Power Stadium and stayed up all night, anxiously waiting to see how it was going to be reported. Once the story emerged, together with the footage, I was absolutely devastated. Plastered across the front page were the words 'England star in racism storm'.

I was embarrassed and asking myself questions that I couldn't answer. How would it affect my family? Would I still have a future at the club? Vichai, our chairman, and Top, his son, had been so good to me from the moment I first met them, and I knew that I'd let them down badly. I thought they'd simply say, 'You're sacked.' I said to Becky, 'I'm done. My career is over.' Because once you've got that tag above your head, that's it. Who's going to want to sign a racist?

By that point we'd already let Shinji Okazaki, the Japan international who had signed for us only six weeks earlier, know about the story. It was obviously a very difficult situation. We hadn't known each other long, but Shinji was incredibly understanding in the circumstances.

I was in the eye of a media storm, and first thing on Sunday morning a statement was released via Leicester to the Press

Association, in which I said, 'I wholeheartedly apologise for any offence I've caused. It was a regrettable error in judgement I take full responsibility for and I accept my behaviour was not up to what's expected of me.'

Leicester also issued their own statement: 'We expect the highest standards from our players on and off the pitch and for them to set an example as role models in our community. We have noted Jamie's apology and will begin a process of investigation into the incident imminently. There will be no further comment until this process has concluded.'

Putting a statement out apologising for my actions immediately was the right thing to do, and I totally supported Leicester's decision. But my personal view is that often with a statement it looks as though you've been told to do it, almost as if you've got to be seen to be doing the right thing. So statements can, when I read them, come across as insincere. And the way I felt was that I didn't just want to do something formal and public, I also wanted to do something private and genuine, because the statement didn't in any way clear my conscience or make me think that everybody could now move on.

I was already aware that the middle-aged man from the casino had got in touch with the club and requested a personal apology from me. He told Jon Rudkin that he had no intention of going to the press, but he said that he wanted to explain his actions and listen to my version of events, and that he expected me to say sorry for how I behaved towards him. It was the least I could do. But I said to the club that I wanted to speak to the students face to face as well. All three people deserved a personal apology, so that they could see that I meant it. Not sorry on paper – sorry when I looked into their eyes.

Everything was organised for us to meet up after training one day. The two students came to the training ground and sat down in Jon Rudkin's office with me and Anthony, the head of media. I explained that I was truly sorry for what I did, and we all shook hands and everything was amicable. I apologised to the middle-aged man separately, and just as sincerely.

It wasn't going to airbrush the episode from history or change the way some people thought about me, but those who had been most affected by the events that night knew how I felt. I think the club recognised the way I responded to the incident when they decided on their own course of action, and I will always be grateful to them, in particular Vichai, for standing by me and recognising that people make mistakes.

A club statement was released on 13 August. It said:

Leicester City Football Club has concluded its investigation into claims made against Jamie Vardy in the national media last weekend. Having established a full account of the incident in question and taken into consideration Jamie's prompt apology, the Club has issued the player with a substantial fine and prescribed a programme of diversity awareness training. Jamie has been reminded of his responsibilities to the Club, his profession and the Leicester community. The fine will be donated to local charities.

I attended two diversity-awareness courses, one through the club, which was for all the players, and another that was set up by the Football Association at Leicester's request purely for myself. The FA course was at Wembley and, hand on heart, I'm really glad that I went along. We had some good, open conversations, about the language around the incident and communication in general.

The tutors explained some of the historical context behind the word and its meaning, dating back to the Second World War, and said that some people would find it offensive and others, specifically those from older generations, may not view it in quite the same way. That discussion definitely opened my eyes and, needless to say, made me feel more embarrassed about what I'd said.

Three-quarters of my fine was allocated to the student I'd offended, to donate to a charity of his choice, and the majority of the rest was distributed through the Foxes Foundation to local charities that Leicester support.

I knew that Leicester's disciplinary action would not be the end of the matter. There was debate in the media about how the FA would handle things in terms of England's code of conduct, and whether I'd be considered for the Euro 2016 qualifiers against San Marino and Switzerland at the start of September.

Roy Hodgson named me in his squad, but he spoke to me as soon as I got to St George's Park, before I'd even had time to put my bag in my room. He said that Dan Ashworth, the FA's technical director, would be speaking to me about my conduct, but there was no way that he wasn't going to name me in the squad. Roy could not have been more supportive, and I really appreciated that. I saw Dan the same day. He asked me to explain what happened and he reminded me of my responsibilities as an England international, on and off the pitch.

That didn't draw a line under everything because I was still turning it over in my mind. So much had been written and said about the incident and our house had been besieged by reporters. It really spelt out just how much my life had changed. And that meant that I needed to change with it because I never again wanted to find myself in a position where my career could be compromised.

I decided to stop going out anywhere and effectively put myself under house arrest, almost like when I was wearing a tag in Malin Bridge (although there was nothing self-imposed about that). So rather than going out for a bit of fun and entertainment, the fun would have to come to our home. I had a bar area built and a full-size snooker table put in a games room, and I spent wild nights putting the children to bed, playing *Call of Duty* and watching *Homeland*.

I just wanted to keep my head down and concentrate on my football, because I was now living in a goldfish bowl, with people watching my every move. A lot of footballers have been able to get used to being in the limelight over time – they've almost grown up with it – but for me it happened in the blink of an eye, and nothing can really prepare you for how it feels. It's like a whirlwind blowing through your life, dragging up anything and everything from your past, leaving you totally unprepared for what might be churned out at any moment in time.

• • •

Nothing is off limits, as I discovered a few months after the casino incident, when I found myself at the centre of another media storm, this time involving my family. First came the story that I'd fallen out with my parents and then, a fortnight later, the *Mail on Sunday* thought it would be a nice idea to let me know that my 'real dad' was someone I didn't know. Not only that, but they sent him down to watch me play and interviewed him about the experience for good measure. For those wondering why I have little time for some people in the media, there's your answer.

The story about the man who left my mum when I was a baby and hadn't made any contact since didn't come from him. It came from the newspaper. They tracked him down and, to make the story 'work', got him to attend a game I was playing in, even though he admitted that he had no interest in football. How the story would affect those involved was of no interest to the *Mail on Sunday*. As far as they were concerned it was their job, their right, to make this public knowledge, irrespective of the pain it would cause.

I only found out about the story a few hours before it was published. I was just about to go on our Christmas night out with the rest of the Leicester players when John, my agent, rang me to break the news in more ways than one. On the back of the family feud article in the *Sun* a couple of weeks earlier, I was starting to feel like it had turned into 'Let's attack Jamie Vardy month'.

'Soccer's record breaker is my son? You're kidding!' was the headline. Underneath, it said: 'Astonishing moment the *MoS* told this man he's the lost father of goalscoring sensation Jamie Vardy'. They also took a photo of him at the stadium, with one arm in the air, and the caption said: 'Richard Gill salutes the son he never knew as Jamie Vardy takes to the field.'

He was saluting the photographer who set the shot up, not me. And, to be clear, I'm no son of his. I've got no intention of ever having him in my life. I scanned the interview that he gave, where he said that he had 'never even heard of Jamie Vardy, let alone realised that he was my son', and he was 'completely overwhelmed and staggered to find out how famous my son is'. I thought, What a prick. I don't want anything to do with him.

I'm sure there would have been a better way to find out that the man I'd called Dad all my life wasn't actually my father. I had a slight inclination that could be the case, because of a few things that happened when I was younger, but it was no more than that. There was one occasion when someone came up to me in the street, saying, 'These are your half brothers.' Another time I was out for a drink in a pub when someone said, 'We know your real dad.' I didn't ask questions or get into a discussion about it, and I didn't share those experiences with anyone. I'm not that sort of person – I keep things to myself. I certainly didn't feel that it was my place to raise it as a subject with my parents. It wasn't as if I was 100 per cent sure, and why should I believe somebody I'd never met before?

I don't know why my parents never sat me down and had the conversation with me. They should have done, because I think I had a right to know. Only they can really answer why they didn't choose to tell me.

I know that John, with the right intentions, tried to get Phil, the dad I'd grown up with, to speak to me on the Saturday night before the story came out, but it didn't happen. We hadn't been on speaking terms for a long time, so there was no appetite for any conversation, let alone on a subject like that.

The falling out with my parents seems to revolve around Becky. There had been no hint of any problem at first. My parents met Becky when we became a couple, and they'd see one another at matches and get on fine. Becky also spent time with Lauren, my sister, who got to know Taylor and Megan.

The first time I realised that there was an issue was when my parents came down to see us with Ella one day. They were quiet and didn't really talk to Becky, which created this awkward atmosphere, and I didn't know what it was all about at the time. Now, I think it all started when Becky came to see me at the pub in the summer of 2014, when I went AWOL for the weekend, and she gave me an ultimatum to sort myself out. That scene ended up getting back to my mum, almost certainly without her knowing the full context.

Everything then came to a head after Sofia was born. My parents felt that I should take Sofia up to see them, rather than them coming down to visit, but there was no way that was going to happen. Sofia was being breastfed, plus she was really ill for the first five or six months, so it was unthinkable for me to have her in the car for a three- or four-hour round trip to Sheffield. Also, it had come to feel as though my parents didn't like Becky.

It reached the stage where my agent got involved to try to sort everything out, and we agreed to meet my mum and dad halfway on 18 December. There was a chance that day for things to get resolved, but then my parents said they couldn't make it. And that was that – any communication was broken off. It means that my parents have never met Sofia, and that obviously saddens me.

Almost a year later the story about the feud surfaced. We knew it was coming because the day before a journalist pressed the buzzer at our home in Melton Mowbray. Becky answered, and the reporter told her that they'd spoken to my family for an article they were running the next day and asked if she wanted to make a comment.

I got straight on the phone to my mum, asking why they'd decided to go to the media. She said that they'd had the press camped outside their house for months, refusing to leave them alone, constantly knocking on the door. And that's what it's like with some newspapers – they'll keep chipping away until you eventually give in. And, unfortunately, my parents did give in. From that moment, the *Sun* knew it could run the story.

When I called my mum that night, my granddad, who had been quoted in the article, came on the phone in tears. He said that the media were forever harassing them, even knocking on his door – a 74-year-old man. Both my granddad and my mum said that they just wanted the reporters to leave them alone, so they'd spoken to them – at the door, not inside their home. I understood how difficult it must have been for them, but no matter how much they were being hounded, they shouldn't have said a word. What was going on had nothing to do with anybody else.

The added frustration for me – and I know that some people will say that this is the price of success and you have to take the rough with the smooth – is that the newspaper could probably have written the same story about 20,000 people in England that weekend. Family rows and break-ups go on everywhere, in all walks of life.

Earlier in the year, before I became an England player, when I had only one Premier League goal to my name, the media wouldn't have been interested in knowing what had gone on between me and my parents. But because I started doing well and my profile increased, it's seen as fair game to write about anything and everything. It was also a good story for them in another sense because it was a chance to knock someone whose career was on the up, and for some reason we enjoy doing that in our country.

When it comes to my family's views on Becky, I think that, as parents, you should be happy with whoever your son or daughter chooses to be with and support them. For some reason my parents didn't see it like that. They didn't agree with the person I wanted to be in my life.

I will always defend Becky. She's had some horrible stuff written about her in the newspapers and it's far from the truth. I know the real Becky, and so do our friends. They can see the difference she's made to my life, both in terms of how my career has benefited massively from the stability she's given me – I'd probably still have that chaotic lifestyle if we'd never met – and also the happiness I feel away from football when I'm with my family.

Nothing else matters when I'm having some cuddles with Sofia or watching her kick a ball about – she takes after her dad already in that sense. I have a lot of fun with Taylor, who occasionally refers to me as Vards and is always talking me into getting on the trampoline with him, and Megan soon worked out that I have my uses when it comes to her maths homework – good old Mr Pemberton again.

Ella lives with her mother in Sheffield, but she's as much a part of my family as the other children and I love seeing her playing with Megan, Taylor and Sofia. They're crackers when they all get together. Unfortunately, it's not been easy to see as much of Ella as I'd like, but that's not for a lack of trying.

I told Emma, Ella's mother, in person that Becky was pregnant, and I could see that she wasn't happy, even though

All smiles at the Grosvenor House Hotel in London, where I attended the PFA Player of the Year dinner and picked up a special award for scoring in 11 consecutive Premier League matches. I was also one of four Leicester players named in the PFA team of the year.

Posing with the Football Writers' Association Footballer of the Year award alongside my agent John Morris, who first started representing me when I was with Halifax in 2011. John told me back then that I'd play for England one day and I couldn't stop laughing. I collected the FWA trophy at the Landmark Hotel in London, three days after we won the title.

© GETTY

© PA IMAGES

'Jamie Vardy's having a party!' The historic moment when Leicester City – 5,000–1 outsiders and relegation favourites – are crowned Premier League champions. All the players had gathered at my house to watch the Chelsea-Spurs match on 2 May.

Who'd have thought it? Aged 29 and less than five years after leaving work at the factory, I've got the Premier League trophy in my hands.

Can you win this every year, Daddy? Sofia, my 19-month-old daughter, enjoys the celebrations on the pitch after we beat Everton 3-1 on the day we were crowned champions.

Another amazing day as nearly 250,000 people line the streets of Leicester, 24 hours after we were given a guard of honour at Chelsea, to see us parade the Premier League trophy, with Claudio, after a bit of encouragement, taking centre stage.

Little did I know what I started when I posted those four words on Facebook in September 2011. A 'Chat Shit Get Banged' T-shirt gets a brief outing during the open-top bus parade.

Sharing a joke with Danny Simpson on stage at Victoria Park, in Leicester, where we were blown away by the crowd that greeted us after we got off the open-top bus.

One of the proudest moments of my career as I come on for Wayne Rooney against the Republic of Ireland in Dublin on 7 June 2015, to win my first England cap. I asked all the England players to sign my shirt afterwards.

'Everything he touches turns to gold,' said Clive Tyldesley, the ITV commentator. A few minutes after coming on against Germany, in March 2016, I scored my first England goal with a back-heel flick from Nathaniel Clyne's cross. 'What just happened there?' was one of the text messages I sent after the game.

My second England cap and my first start for my country, against San Marino at Stadio Olimpico on 5 September 2015. We won 6–0 on a pitch that was worse than anything I played on at non-league level – not that I was complaining. I love wearing that three lions shirt.

Jumping for joy in France. Another goal for England after coming off the bench, this time an equaliser against Wales in Lens, in the Euro 2016 group game that we won 2–1. After scoring I ran straight to James Milner, who became one of my closest friends in the England squad.

And look who was in the stadium to see it happen – my best mates from Sheffield who are known as 'the Inbetweeners' and have followed me everywhere since my non-league days. From left to right: Grant, Collins, Ridgey and Rans. Phil, Grant's uncle, (far right), travelled around France with them.

At Ocean Beach Club in Ibiza in the summer of 2015, enjoying a drink or two with Becky, Gary Taylor-Fletcher and his wife, Andy King, Chris Wood and a few others.

Beer o'clock in Dubai with Danny Drinkwater and Matty James as we enjoy a well-earned mid-season break in February 2016. Claudio gave us a week off after losing against Arsenal and most of the team booked into the same resort with their families for some sunshine … and the odd beverage.

'Looking for some inspiration for your speech, Nuge?' David Nugent was the best man at my wedding. He was the first person to introduce himself when I walked in the Leicester dressing room and from then we hit it off.

Exchanging vows at Peckforton Castle, in Cheshire, on 25 May 2016. I never thought I'd get married but within six months of meeting Becky I proposed and two years later we tied the knot.

The wedding was a perfect day, shared with our closest friends, including a number of my Leicester teammates and Vichai, the club's owner and his son 'Top'.

Enjoying some quiet time on the River Soar, near our old house in Mountsorrel, where I taught Megan and Taylor how to fish. I also had a few issues with a goose.

Sofia, on holiday in the summer of 2015, shows why she was the obvious choice to be a flower girl at our wedding the following year.

Some welcome chill out time with the family in Turks and Caicos just after winning my first cap for England. Becky and the children mean everything to me.

we hadn't been together for several years. It felt as though things got more difficult from that point in terms of access, especially on the back of the falling out with my parents, because there was a time when they would bring Ella to every home game at Leicester and she would stay over with me.

I make sure that Ella is looked after financially, but I want to see her as well. The time I can spend with Ella is restricted, and it's not easy because weekends are tricky, for obvious reasons, with matches kicking off at all sorts of times. If I'm playing away from home, or it's a Sunday match, it's not straightforward. I can't do a long drive to Sheffield and back the day before a game – clubs have rules about that kind of thing, which is understandable. So Becky usually picks Ella up and we try to provide as many options as possible so that I can maintain my relationship with her.

We FaceTime regularly, and she makes me smile with some of the things she comes out with. She once said to me, 'Someone at school asked me if I was famous, Daddy.' I asked her why and she replied, 'They know you play football, so they think I'm famous as well.'

There's such innocence behind that comment, but I do hope that my children can grow up in an environment where every move they make isn't a headline.

For me, it's a spotlight that comes with the territory, and I certainly wouldn't change a thing about the way my football career has panned out. Yet there are times when it becomes a bit much, and I wish I could go back to those days when I was so anonymous that I could get away with playing a match under somebody else's name.

11

'MAY THE PORT BE WITH YOU'

Becky pointed to the USB stick on the side in the kitchen. 'You need to take a look at that,' she said.

I glanced at her curiously, wondering what was going on. It was Friday 27 November and I'd just got back from training. The next day we were playing Manchester United, and I knew that the eyes of the world were going to be on me to see if I could break Ruud van Nistelrooy's record and become the first player to score in 11 successive Premier League matches. I was excited but mentally drained. The media coverage had reached saturation point. Everybody wanted to ask me about the record. I understood that, of course, but I also felt like I'd done enough interviews to last a lifetime.

I turned on the laptop, plugged in the USB stick and sat back, not knowing what to expect. A video came on that started with footage of me on the day that I signed for Leicester, standing in the middle of the pitch at the King Power Stadium, holding a scarf and wearing the oversized top from the club shop. Over the top of the images I could hear me talking in the interview I gave to Anthony, Leicester's head of media, on that same May day in 2012 when everything felt so new: 'Well, it's obviously going to be a big step, but I think that I can do it in myself.'

Then it cut to me sitting in the dugout, where Anthony and I were talking. I was 25, unshaven and with a crew cut, yet to kick a ball in professional football and trying to explain what I'd bring to Leicester. 'Obviously, I want to contribute as much as I can and hopefully we'll be in the Premier League,' I said. 'I always give 110 per cent, a lot of hard work, I won't stop running. Hopefully, the goals will come.'

All the memories came flooding back. Kodaline's 'Love Will Set You Free' was playing as I watched myself in action for Leicester: sliding a shot the wrong side of an upright, scoring goals, sprinting flat-out, making tackles, hugging teammates, having a laugh – a snapshot of life at the club. I just assumed that the video was going to continue in the same way, but then, to my amazement, players, staff, the manager – even my fiancée and my agent – started to appear one after the other, talking into the camera.

'Jamie Vardy,' said Jeff Schlupp, breaking into laughter.

'You should be immensely proud,' Kasper added. 'We back you all the way to beat the record here against Man United.'

'You've created history already, and whether you beat the record or not this Saturday, mate, you've done it already in our eyes,' Jeff said.

'A fantastic achievement, not only for you but for the football club,' said Shakey, one of Claudio's assistants. 'But for you personally, I'm really chuffed for you.'

'From where you started and where you are now … massive congratulations, absolutely bossing it,' Drinky said.

'What happens tomorrow doesn't really matter now,' Kingy said. 'To have surpassed some of the names you've gone past to get that record, and to be equal with an outstanding player like Van Nistelrooy, is absolutely brilliant.'

'An amazing achievement,' Marc Albrighton said. 'All the best for Saturday. I hope you break the record because you deserve it.'

'If you don't do it, it doesn't matter,' said Alan Birchenhall, a former Leicester player turned ambassador for the club. 'It's what you've contributed to our football club. It's a fairytale, and it's fantastic.'

'I really hope that you break the record on Saturday. All the best, pal,' Matty James added.

'I wish you all the best for Saturday. I hope you can do it. And may the port be with you,' Paul McAndrew, the kitman, said.

'I hope for you that you're going to score on Saturday. But if we have a penalty, I'm going to take it,' said Riyad, smiling.

'Keep it going,' Wes said. 'One more to be the all-out record holder. We all believe in you. We all know that you can do it. Good luck!'

Then it cut back to Riyad. 'Nah, I'm only joking,' he added, laughing.

'Congratulations,' said Dave Rennie, the physio. 'You've obviously kept us busy with your wrists and your groin and everything else.'

'We're all very proud of you for what you've achieved,' Ritchie said.

'I know you'll be bang on it, totally focused,' John, my agent, added.

'It's not important if you achieve or not achieve,' Claudio said. 'It's important what you did.'

'In Thailand, you said to me that you're going to repay everything that I did for you. Today, you already did that,' Top, the vice-chairman, said.

'And no matter what happens this weekend, you're an inspiration to your teammates and so many people out there, so congratulations,' Becky said, with a big smile across her face.

Then came the goals that had taken me to the verge of creating history, ending with the one I scored against Newcastle at St James' Park the previous Saturday. 'Jamie Vardy, away from his man and he's scored! It's the Premier League record-equalling goal,' said the commentator, as the video finished with Wes lifting me up in the air in celebration.

Wow. I was totally blown away. It was brilliantly put together – full credit to the media lads – and really thoughtful. I couldn't believe that they'd managed to pull it off – all those interviews at the training ground, including one with Becky – without me having the faintest idea that anything was going on.

I enjoyed every bit of the video but one comment in particular really made me laugh, and that was Macca's line 'may the port be with you', which was a subtle reference to a superstition I'd picked up at the start of the season. I can't say why it started, because I genuinely don't know, but I decided to drink a glass of port on the eve of every game in the 2015–16 season. I've always enjoyed port, especially if it's a decent one, like a 30-year-old Tawny, and, although I'm not normally superstitious, from the moment I scored against Sunderland on the opening day, I didn't want to change anything.

I'd fill a small plastic water or Lucozade bottle to halfway and just sip the port while watching TV. It tastes like Ribena to me, and it helps me switch off and get to sleep a bit easier the night before a game. I told Dave Rennie what I was doing, and he took the view that if it works for me and I'm scoring goals, then fair enough.

That wasn't the only change to my preparation that season. Under Nigel we had to report an hour and a half before a home game, but Claudio wanted us all to eat together at the King Power Stadium prior to the match, which meant coming in three-and-a-half hours before kick-off. Everybody was fine with that, provided we had a room to chill out in after we'd had our food. So we had what I like to think of as a secret players' lounge put in at the King Power Stadium.

You go through a set of double doors from the eating area into it, and there are loads of TVs, reclining chairs, corner sofas, a PlayStation, dartboard and pool table. Some of the lads would bring their laptops and iPads so that they could sit back and watch a series they'd downloaded, while a few of the other boys, such as Riyad, N'Golo and Danny Simpson, liked to sleep at that time, so there's a separate area in an adjacent room with some beds.

As for me, with a can of Red Bull and a double espresso inside me, there's no chance I'm putting my head on the pillow. As soon as I walk in, I go straight to the corner with the pool table and dartboard. It's no expense spared in that room, apart from when it comes to the games area. The pool table's got a slant on it – you've got to know the slope to have any chance – and one of the cues is bent. But a workman should never blame his tools, so we happily get on with it and the times flies by.

The week before my record-breaking goalscoring run started, we drew 1–1 at home with Tottenham and the lads weren't happy. We showed them far too much respect, letting them have the ball out wide where they were pummelling crosses in. Our performance was far too passive and we felt that we should have got at them more.

The plan was to put that right at Bournemouth, but we fell behind to an overhead kick from Callum Wilson. We looked to be heading for our first defeat of the season until Steve Cook brought me down in the area in the 86th minute. Riyad was our designated penalty taker, but he'd been taken off at half-time. Leo would normally be next in line but he was on the bench, so we ended up with this strange situation where I was stood around asking who was going to take it.

Nobody wanted to except for Joe Dodoo, a 20-year-old academy graduate who was only 15 minutes into his Premier League debut. Full marks to Joe for his confidence, but I remember saying to him at the time that I couldn't let him put the ball on the spot because I was worried that he'd get loads of stick if he missed, and I didn't think that was fair for someone whose career was just starting. So in the absence of any better ideas – and with Kingy also encouraging me – I stepped forward.

I took a fairly straight run up and just thought I'd smash it to the right as hard as I could. Artur Boruc in goal got his hand to it, but there was too much pace on the ball. It was strange because the night before the match our Polish centre-half Marcin Wasilewski, who knows Boruc, told me that he was very good at saving penalties. It didn't cross my mind when I stepped up, but it did as soon as I ran off celebrating. I didn't miss the opportunity to remind 'Was' as soon as I got on the coach afterwards. 'Too strong for him, Was,' I said, laughing.

• • •

In the international break that followed I made my first England start in a 6–0 away win against San Marino, on a day when Wayne Rooney equalled Sir Bobby Charlton's goalscoring record. The surface was horrendous, and one of the reporters, reflecting on my non-league days, wrote that 'if anyone should have been at home on the vegetable patch that passed for a pitch in San Marino, it was Jamie Vardy'. To be clear, that pitch was worse than anything I ever played on at Stocksbridge, Halifax or Fleetwood. It was almost as if a car park had been sprayed green, because it was like playing on gravel.

Roy started me on the left-hand side of a three-man attack, with Harry Kane through the middle. I thought that I put a good shift in, but I was disappointed not to get on the scoresheet and I ended the game with two massive lumps on my head. I jumped up with Cristian Brolli, one of their centre-halves, and headed him instead of the ball, so he had to wear a bandage. About five minutes later I did exactly the same thing with the opposite side of my head on Brolli again.

That second England call-up led to us changing our wedding date. We'd originally planned to get married on 4 June 2016, which we booked back in January 2015, not thinking for a moment that the European Championship finals would come into the equation. Becky got a bit nervous about things when I was first named in the England squad, but I told her to stop worrying, so we left it. When I was involved with England again I started to see where she was coming from. We looked into getting married the first week after the end of the season, but Leicester didn't think that was a great idea because of their commitments, namely the annual trip to Thailand. So we decided to go for 25 May because there were no other dates available.

Although I was starting to feel more comfortable around the England set-up, I certainly wasn't taking anything for granted. I knew I had to keep scoring goals at club level. I managed to do that in a 3–2 win over Aston Villa on 13 September, when we came back from 2–0 down with less than half an hour to go to maintain our unbeaten start. If ever a game summed up what we were about as a team at Leicester, the one against Villa was it. It didn't matter what obstacle was in front of us, we'd always carry on to the end. 'Foxes never quit' is the slogan above the tunnel at the King Power Stadium, and we followed that to the letter.

Ritchie pulled a goal back to reduce the deficit, and when Drinky delivered a low cross from the right ten minutes later, nothing was going to stop me getting on the end of it. I saw the space behind Joleon Lescott, and as Leandro Bacuna came across to try to block me I didn't take my eye off the ball. Bacuna ended up in a heap, goalkeeper Brad Guzan was beaten and I was sliding on my knees in celebration. At that stage the game had been totally turned on its head. The momentum was with us as Nathan Dyer, making his first appearance after joining on loan from Swansea, bravely nodded in the winner to complete the turnaround.

The only thing that took the edge off the game for me was an injury I picked up in the first half when Micah Richards tackled me as I was running. He got the ball, but as I fell over my hand landed flat and my wrist bent over the top of it. I didn't know what I'd done at the time, but I knew I had a problem. At half-time I went over to Dave Rennie and told him that it wasn't right, but I made it clear that there was no way I was coming off. He put a strapping on it to keep it as stable as possible.

The following day, I rang Dave to say that I thought it could be something serious, so I had an X-ray which showed that two different bones were fractured in my wrist – the scaphoid and the triquetrum. I should have had an operation there and then, but it would have meant being out for six to eight weeks, which I wasn't prepared to do, especially as I'd had that second England call-up and things were going so well with Leicester. So I had a splint made up and the consultant said it was fine for me to play as long as I had it on. He did explain, though, that we would have to consider surgery if the bones didn't heal.

By now Claudio had been in charge for a couple of months and he'd got to know us all pretty well, as personalities as well as players. One day, because I was doing my usual thing of rabbiting on in the dressing room, he told me to turn the radio off. I just looked at him, confused, and Claudio said, 'You, you're always talking. You're like fucking radio. You, radio wanker!' My new nickname was coined.

Later in the season Wes said to the media that 'the relationship the gaffer has got with Vards is the best – there's a lot of swearing involved, they both give as good as they get'. I learned a few Italian phrases from Andrea Azzalin, the fitness coach Claudio brought with him to the club, but I don't throw them all at the manager. I'll say *bastardo* when he calls me by my nickname, and we both have a laugh about it, but I know that I can't go too far with it. He is the gaffer, after all.

As a group of players we all warmed to Claudio the person as well as Claudio the manager. He's coached some top clubs, so you can't dispute his record, but he's also got the ability to laugh at himself, whether he's searching for the right word in English – sometimes with the help of one of the players – or coming out with one of his little catchphrases. 'Dilly-ding, dilly-dong', his imaginary bell, came out early in the season whenever he thought one of the lads was not paying attention, and as soon as he said it we all started doing the same. There are times when you don't know whether Claudio is being funny or not, like during warm-ups when you have to open your groins out. Claudio will be standing there watching, and all of a sudden you'll hear him shout, 'Open very well. Your groins, not mine!' You can't help but smile and think, Where on earth did that come from?

There was a sense of déjà vu about the trip to Stoke on the back of beating Villa, because we found ourselves chasing the game once again. We were 2–0 down inside 20 minutes, and not many teams would get a result at the Britannia Stadium from that position. But Riyad levelled from the spot and then set up the equaliser for me in the most unlikely fashion. The ball was pumped forward and I just gambled, hoping that Riyad would win a header – something that he had hardly ever done before. Both centre-halves were drawn to the ball and Riyad managed to flick it on and that left me free. I held off Erik Pieters with my broken wrist and steered the ball past Jack Butland in the Stoke goal.

That was three in three for me, and four in the first six games, but all I could think about was how well the season had started for the team. We were fourth in the table and the only unbeaten side in the league, but nobody was getting carried away. Claudio said at the start of the season that he just wanted us to get to the safety zone – 40 points – as quickly as possible, and that was the only target.

In many ways we saw Arsenal's visit in the next game as a free hit, because nobody expects you to win those matches. Arsenal beat us by doing what we did to other teams – hitting your opponent on the counter-attack. Alexis Sanchez scored a hat-trick and we lost 5–2, but it could easily have ended up 6–5.

I scored twice, the first after coming short and spinning in behind, because I knew I was up against Per Mertesacker and that there would be space to run into once I had turned. Drinky picked me out with a pass – you'll read that sentence a lot – I nodded it on and nobody came to close me down, so I opened up my body and bent the ball into the far corner. By the time I got my second, in the 89th minute, Arsenal were out of sight.

The big question for us was how we would react, because we were conscious of how things had unravelled for us at a similar stage the previous season. A 2–1 win at Norwich on

3 October showed our mental strength, and I scored for the fifth successive game, courtesy of a penalty after Sébastien Bassong had gone into the back of me. Riyad had been left out, so once again I stepped up to take the spot-kick.

With the opposition analysis that is put together for us to download on our iPads, we get to see where the penalty taker normally puts his kicks, and I knew that Norwich would probably do the same sort of research on us. So I decided to whip rather than blast the penalty, to the opposite side to the one I took at Bournemouth. John Ruddy, the Norwich keeper, dived the wrong way and we were in front.

Opposition analysis has always been a big thing during my time at Leicester, but Claudio is absolutely meticulous. He knows everything about the team we're coming up against, right down to the number of times their right-winger has crossed it with his right foot and his left – that's how deep he goes into it. He'd go through it all in the meeting room at the training ground, and we'd get together like that at least twice a week. Everything is available to download on our iPads two days before each game, and the analysis covers every opposition player, as well as how the team have taken their last 20 corners and those penalty kicks for Kasper.

In the end we won 2–1 at Norwich, with Jeff Schlupp scoring a second just after half-time, but there was a horrible moment when I thought my season was over. I jumped for the ball, and as I came down I badly jarred my knee. I needed treatment for several minutes and the medical staff could see that I was concerned. I genuinely feared I'd done something to my cruciate ligament. Luckily, it was OK, and Claudio confirmed after the match that I'd be fit enough to join up with England for the Euro 2016 qualifiers against Estonia and Lithuania.

• • •

The Estonia match was my first visit to Wembley since I went to see Sheffield Wednesday lose to Arsenal in the 1993 FA Cup final replay, and obviously the stadium had changed a bit since then. I was on the bench and didn't come on until the 83rd minute, but I set up a goal almost straight away, which was a brilliant feeling. I probably could have shot but Raheem Sterling was in a better position to score, and in that situation I'd always pass. I've always been proud of my number of assists, not just my goals.

Three days later I was in the starting 11 in Lithuania, in a game played on artificial turf. It was like my trial at Crewe all over again. I knocked the ball past a defender and I couldn't bloody catch it. Roy played me wide, and there was a bit of a media debate afterwards about whether I should have got a chance through the middle. I wasn't worried about that – I was just pleased to be playing. I thought I did myself justice, but there was also this nagging frustration in my head that I'd made four appearances for England and still hadn't scored.

There was no such problem at club level. The trip to Southampton on 17 October followed a familiar pattern as we went 2–0 behind and fought back to salvage a point. I got both goals, the first a near-post header from a superb cross by Nathan Dyer, who'd come off the bench at half-time along with Riyad to give us fresh impetus. After squandering a decent chance to equalise, I wasn't going to waste another one when Riyad put me through in the 90th minute. I actually wanted him to release me earlier, when I knew that I was 100 per cent onside, but he took another touch. Luckily, the right-back played me on, and I put my foot through the ball to make it 2–2. By now my confidence was sky-high, and the way we kept coming back – we'd already picked up seven points from losing positions – said so much for our never-say-die attitude in the squad.

N'Golo Kanté, who began the season on the bench, made his fifth Premier League start against Southampton, and by then we could all see that he was a special player as well as a lovely lad. We got a clear idea of what N'Golo was like as a person not long after he signed. The club leaves the players to police the fine system, and if you fail to arrive on time it's £100. If it happens twice in the same week, the fine doubles. When we were explaining to him one day that he had to pay up because he was late – which was taking a while because his English wasn't great – he turned round to us and said, 'How can I pay that fine when there are people in Africa starving?' And that is N'Golo all over. He would much rather give that £100 to people who genuinely need it. And what could we say in response to that?

He's such a humble man. When he first signed he didn't think he'd need a car. He said he would walk to training. But he got himself a Mini, and that car became his pride and joy. Every day he'd come in with a big smile on his face, say, 'Good morning,' shake everyone's hand and quietly get on with his day.

On the pitch the guy never stops running. He could finish games and, I'm sure, do another 90 minutes. He just never looks tired. But it's not just the distance he covers, with N'Golo it's the number of high-speed intensity runs that he does to win the ball back. In training we'd do a keep-ball box, with eleven of us around the outside and two in the middle, and I started to think that N'Golo was deliberately giving it away because getting it back was so much fun for him.

We'd made a brilliant start to the season, exceeding everybody's expectations, but if there was one thing we needed to put right it was the absence of a clean sheet. That changed when we beat Palace 1–0, and Claudio stayed true to his promise to take us all out for a pizza as a reward. Except it wasn't quite what we had in mind. When we got to Peter Pizzeria in the city centre we discovered that we had to make our own pizzas from scratch, so you can imagine how quickly it started to get messy. Pizza dough was being thrown everywhere. It turned into another good team-bonding afternoon, and made a nice change from the Domino's deliveries I'd once lived off.

My goal in the Palace game came about because of a mistake from Brede Hangeland, who could have passed the ball anywhere but gifted it to Riyad. The previous week, when Palace played West Ham at home, I watched the highlights on *Match of the Day* and saw West Ham's Dimitri Payet go through in a similar position. He faked to shoot and Palace keeper Wayne Hennessey went down, so Payet just lifted it over him. So when I found myself one-on-one with Hennessey, following Riyad's perfect first-time pass, I did the same as Payet, but instead of shooting I dinked it over Hennessey and, because Scott Dann was still trying to get back, I made sure that I followed the ball in and smashed it into the back of the net as hard as I could. That was my tenth Premier League goal of the season, and when I celebrated I held up both hands and counted every finger, just to let everyone know that I'd doubled my tally from the Great Escape campaign.

The media were reporting that I'd become only the fifth Englishman to score in seven successive Premier League matches, but it wasn't until the week after, at West Brom, that talk of individual records started to enter my head. Ruud van Nistelrooy's name was brought up, and I had no idea until then that he held the Premier League record by scoring in ten successive matches. I was a bit surprised that someone like Alan Shearer hadn't gone on a longer run, given all the goals he scored.

With less than 15 minutes to go against West Brom, I started to think that it wasn't going to be my day. We were leading 2–1 through a couple of goals from Riyad, who was on fire, and time was running out for me to score. But then we hit them on the counter. I laid it off to Drinky, spinning Jonny Evans at the same time, and got the return pass. There was still a way to go, but it seemed like the West Brom defenders had caravans on their backs as I ran through with my afterburners firing again. I slotted it away to make it eight in a row, and at the final whistle I stood on the pitch listening to our fans singing 'Jamie Vardy, he scores when he wants'. What a moment. And what a change from a year earlier, when I was stuck on one goal.

In the post-match interviews people started talking about me being in an elite club, along with Daniel Sturridge and Van Nistelrooy, who had scored in eight successive Premier League matches, but I was more concerned with what I was going to wear that night. It was Halloween and I'd promised to take the kids out for a bit of trick-or-treating.

Sam Bailey, *The X Factor* winner, invited us over to her house – she's a big Leicester fan who we'd got to know well – and I had a choice between dressing up as the Grim Reaper or a clown. I went for the Grim Reaper in the end, but the mask was so hot that I couldn't keep it on, and a few people noticed that it was me when we knocked on their door.

Someone got annoyed that I wouldn't pose for a photo on their doorstep and they put something on social media to that effect, which really pissed me off. It's at times like that, when I'm having some fun with my children and doing the same as parents all over the country, that I just want to be their dad. I wasn't the Premier League's leading scorer that night. I was just a 28-year-old bloke taking his kids trick-or-treating on Halloween. Don't get me wrong, I'll sign autographs and have my picture taken whenever I can, because I've been a football fan and appreciate what those moments mean to supporters. But now and again, and in particular when I'm with my family, I like a little bit of personal space, for my children as much as anyone. I don't want them to grow up with a dad who breaks off from everything he does with them to have his picture taken.

● ● ●

Life was a joy on the pitch. I was playing with so much inner belief that I thought I'd score every time I crossed the white line. Watford were our next opponents, and I was just hoping for one clear opportunity. We were leading 1–0 through N'Golo's toe-poke when Heurelho Gomes, the Watford keeper, cleaned me out in the area. Riyad was on the pitch this time, but I hoped he would step aside. I asked him politely, pointing out that we were winning at the time anyway, but Riyad wanted to take it, so I just left him to it. Then, all of a sudden, the crowd started booing. Riyad turned around and gave me the ball. I wasn't thinking placement – I just blasted it down the middle. And the first thing I did afterwards was point in Riyad's direction and embrace him, because I appreciated what he'd done for me there.

My scoring run stood at nine consecutive games. But there was a problem. At the end of the Watford match I was struggling with my groin. Nothing showed up on the scan, so I joined up with England for the friendlies against Spain and France in November, although the FA knew that I was carrying an injury. I started training the day before the Spain game but only lasted about five minutes, because there was something there, still niggling and quite painful. I stayed in Spain and watched the match, then I went back to Leicester and just wanted to get it sorted straight away.

We went back to see David Lloyd, the consultant surgeon who'd dealt with the groin problems I had in the promotion-winning season. He felt that a lot of the discomfort was around the inguinal ligament, almost like a hernia problem, rather than any recurrence of what I'd had previously. Surgery was mentioned but I was never going to go down that path. So David suggested a one-off cortisone injection directly into the ligament, which usually takes about seven to ten days to work. I needed mine to start working within four days. I wasn't missing the Newcastle game for anything. I'd have chopped my leg off and grabbed a crutch if I'd had to – there was just no way I wasn't going to be on the pitch.

I've got to give huge credit to Dave Rennie for getting me into the sort of condition where I could play, because when I came back from Spain it looked highly unlikely. The cryotherapy chamber at Leicester's training ground also helped because I was in there every day, twice a day, in the lead-up to the Newcastle match. It's a seven-metre long unit that cost the club £150,000 and has been worth every penny in helping with players' recovery and rehabilitation from injuries.

Once inside, you have to wear shorts, long socks with a pair of thermal slippers, protective mittens, a headband to cover your ears, a respiratory mask and a compression bandage around your kneecaps and elbows, because that's where the skin is thinnest. You go into a pre-chamber that's set to −65 to 70°C, and after about 30 seconds a green light comes on. Then you go through to another room, and that's where the temperature falls to as low as minus 135 degrees. You spend three to five minutes in there, no more than that, and as a way of passing the time I'd often sing along to some ballads with a couple of the lads. Danny Simpson, Marc Albrighton and I have been known to belt out 'I Don't Want to Miss a Thing' by Aerosmith. It's a good thing our ears are covered.

As I got towards the end of that week I was feeling much better, and a message on the eve of the Newcastle match gave me even more encouragement. Ruud van Nistelrooy posted on his Instagram account: 'Records are there to be broken... Go on @vardy7, all the best and good luck!'

St James' Park was where Van Nistelrooy had set the record back in 2003, so everyone was saying that it was written in the stars for me to equal it. And, to be honest, I think the lads were so desperate for me to do it that they were trying to put me through whenever possible. Then, on the stroke of half-time, it came together. I picked up the ball wide on the left and played it inside to Leo. Fabricio Coloccini didn't follow me, Leo picked me out with a deft pass, and I cut inside Moussa Sissoko and gambled that Rob Elliot, the Newcastle keeper, would think I would try to go across him, so I went for the near post. *Bang!* The ball fizzed inside the upright and I'd done it – I'd equalled Van Nistelrooy's record. I wheeled away, blowing kisses to the Leicester fans behind the goal and soaking it all in as Wes came over and picked me up.

There was a lovely moment later in the game, when I was substituted with 13 minutes to go and the Newcastle supporters applauded. They didn't have to do that. They were 2–0 down at the time and must have been pretty fed up with the way the game was going, but they showed a touch of class that day and I'll never forget it.

Claudio made a point of thanking the Newcastle fans in his press conference, moments after he'd put me on the spot in the dressing room when he asked me to do a speech. There was a bit of applause from everyone as I stood up and tried to think of what to say.

'Cheers, boys,' I said. 'I wouldn't have been able to do it without all of you, and the gaffer's just said he's going to put some beers on the coach and the plane for us.' And, to be fair to Claudio, he did let us have one beer each on the way home.

I left with the match ball under my arm, which normally only happens if you score a hat-trick. At the end of the game I'd gone back onto the pitch to shake the opposition players' hands, and Mike Jones, the referee, told me to knock on his door when I got down the tunnel and he'd give me the ball for equalling the record. I really appreciated that and got all the lads to sign it for me.

Although I was getting all the headlines, I saw myself as a chapter in a much bigger story that was unfolding. The 3–0 win at Newcastle lifted us to the top of the table, and we were playing with such belief, right throughout the team. It felt as though we had the perfect blend of characters. Everything was relaxed, we were just enjoying ourselves and even Kasper, who's so driven and focused, was having a laugh and a joke.

Still, there was no escaping the spotlight that was on me for the time being, and the fact that we were playing against United next – a top-of-the-table clash with Van Nistelrooy's old club – only increased the level of interest.

Nike were hoping that I'd wear some gold boots to mark the occasion. Normally, I'd like a week with a new pair of boots before playing in them. I usually get in the bath with them on, so that they mould to my feet, and then wear them in training for four days before a match. But the gold boots only arrived on the Thursday, which wasn't ideal.

In the lead-up to the match I got the feeling that everybody was willing me to break the record, so much so that I could sense some people were a bit concerned about how I'd feel if it didn't happen. On the night before the United game I got a phone call from my agent.

'Don't worry if you don't get one,' John said.

'Don't worry. I will,' I replied.

I wasn't being arrogant. It's just that when you've gone that far, and you get that close to creating history, you expect to do it. Entertaining doubt isn't going to do you any good.

Plus, I'd had another glass of port, so there was nothing to worry about.

I'd also had a local-anaesthetic jab in my groin so that I'd be pain-free in a game where I knew I'd have my work cut out. Chris Smalling, who I've played with for England, is without doubt my toughest opponent. He's like a rash, all over you, and you can't get away from him. If the ball comes into you, he's tight, and often the only pass you've got on is backwards.

I needed to find a way to lose Chris and, thankfully, United did that for me. They had a corner in the 24th minute and he went up to try to score. I was just about the only Leicester player not defending and took up a position wide on the left. Kasper caught the corner and rolled it out to Christian Fuchs, who'd starting running into space on the right, deep inside our half. Once Christian started carrying it forward I knew that I had to try to shuffle across the pitch. Ashley Young had a little tug of my arm as I darted across him, but that wasn't going to stop me. Sensing that there was a chance I could get in on goal, I pointed to where I wanted the ball, in behind Matteo Darmian, and Christian played an unbelievable pass, perfectly weighted.

Now it was me against David de Gea, just as it had been 14 months earlier in that mad 5–3 win at the King Power Stadium. There was hardly any time to think, but it's amazing what can go through your mind in a split second. I could picture that strange De Gea stance before I shot, and more than anything I was thinking, Don't fucking miss.

I took a touch and then with one swing of my right boot – and a golden boot at that – De Gea was beaten and the record was mine. The noise inside the King Power Stadium was deafening, and the adrenaline rush took over, carrying me along the side of the pitch and past the United fans, who'd been singing Ruud van Nistelrooy's name non-stop. 'Me, me – all fucking me,' I shouted as I ran past them, jabbing a finger into my chest. You're not in control in moments like that. Nothing's choreographed – it's just raw emotion.

One of the things I enjoy about watching that goal back is seeing what it meant to our whole team. That was no ordinary celebration. Players came running from everywhere – bear in mind that we'd been defending a corner a few seconds earlier – and Claudio was emotional on the touchline. I was mobbed by everyone – well, almost everyone. Huthy couldn't be arsed to run all the way over to the far corner of the ground, and he went to the dugout and had a drink instead.

Later that night I turned on the TV and Bastian Schweinsteiger was talking about me in the same breath as Miroslav Klose, Germany's record goalscorer – it was absolute madness. My phone was vibrating constantly, and it wasn't until the next morning that I started to go through the messages. One of the tweets was from Danny Care, who was in the same Sheffield

Wednesday Under-15 team as me but quit football to take up rugby and go on to play scrum-half for Harlequins and England – an amazing story. 'Taught him everything he knows', Danny said underneath a photo of us in that Wednesday side. We're back in touch now and often have a chuckle about the way things have turned out for us both, because Danny was also told by Wednesday that he was too small.

The message that meant the most to me was the one I received from Ruud van Nistelrooy: 'Well done @vardy7! You're number one now and you deserved it #11inarow.' To read that from the main man, someone I used to watch on *Match of the Day* when I was playing non-league football, was incredible.

As for Claudio, he was also chuffed to bits, and he presented me with a signed Leicester shirt at the training ground a few days later. I turned it round to look at the back. It said '9. Wanker'.

12

'THE WHOLE TEAM
IS CAESAR'

We all agreed that we would meet in the hotel reception at 11am. But Batman, Assassin's Creed, Bananaman and the white Power Ranger – Robert Huth, Ritchie de Laet, Shinji Okazaki and Jamie Vardy, to give us our real names – were being kept waiting and getting a bit impatient.

It was our Christmas party in Copenhagen, the theme was computer-game characters and we'd all promised to keep our outfits secret, so there was a sense of excitement when people started coming down the stairs at our hotel. Wes, our captain, stole the show dressed as a giant Pac-Man.

Andrej Kramarić was Bowser, Danny Simpson Spiderman, Kasper Schmeichel Mr Incredible, Jeff Schlupp the black Power Ranger and Nathan Dyer Iron Man. The Teenage Mutant

Ninja Turtles – Matty James, Andy King, Ben Hamer and Danny Drinkwater – had strength in numbers, but there was an obvious drawback that they'd overlooked when choosing their costumes. They had to take their heads off to be able to drink. One way or another, though, we all found a way to get the pints of Guinness down us that Sunday.

It was the morning after the night before. A night when I was doing chin-ups in a bar – not something you'd ever see me doing in a gym – Shinji never got off the dance floor and a group of lads who'd become incredibly close celebrated a 3–0 win at Swansea that took us to the top of the Premier League.

Claudio had agreed to give us Sunday and Monday off after the 'committee' – Wes, Kasper and Kingy – successfully put forward our case for a bit of festive fun. Every so often I get rolled out as the fourth member of that union, generally when they need someone to tell it how it is.

Unfortunately, our hopes of staying under the radar in Copenhagen, and enjoying a laugh without the media following our every move, went up in smoke after Andrej, quite innocently, posted a picture of us on Instagram. By the time we sat down for dinner at the Winter Wonderland in Tivoli Gardens, where our fancy dress costumes led some people to think that we actually worked at the amusement park, photographers were waiting around every corner.

We ended up getting smuggled out, via tunnels, a lift – some of the lads got stuck in it – up and down staircases, into something that resembled a bunker, and then all of a sudden we were on the main street and diving into the taxi waiting for us. There was a tinge of disappointment that it wasn't a Batmobile.

A few hours later I was boarding a private plane back to East Midlands airport because the story about my 'real dad' had broken, and people back home – in particular Becky and my agent John – were worried that the media knew where to find me and that it could turn into a circus for everyone else. The first I knew of my early departure was when Ritchie, my room-mate, woke me up after I'd fallen asleep at our hotel late on Sunday afternoon.

'Come on, we're going,' he said, packing up our stuff.

'Going where?' I replied.

'To the airport. We've got a plane home,' said Ritchie, who'd been briefed on the situation.

And that was it. Jon Sanders, the player liaison officer, put us in a taxi together and we entered Copenhagen airport through a back entrance, where my most expensive plane ticket ever – about £20,000 – got us back to Leicester while the lads were partying in Denmark. I sent them a text just before we took off – 'Enjoy the rest of the Christmas do, boys, I'm not going to let the papers turn up and spoil it for everyone' – and word has it that while I was tucked up in bed in Melton Mowbray, catching up on my sleep, Shinji was putting in another epic performance on the dance floor in Copenhagen.

• • •

In many ways a weekend spent in Wales and Denmark reinforced what we already knew about our Leicester side. Everyone was playing with supreme confidence and we had incredible team spirit – a winning combination at any level.

My record-breaking run had come to an end at Swansea, where Riyad was flying and scored a hat-trick. But there was a positive – I didn't have to do any more interviews trotting out the same lines about the same subject. Everybody must have been tired of hearing my voice, and it was a relief for me when the media department promised to leave me alone for a month.

Nine days after Swansea I was back among the goals against Chelsea at the King Power Stadium, where Walkers were handing out Vardy Salted Crisps – another of those moments when you shake your head at the madness of it all.

I was bang up for Chelsea's visit, fuelled in part by a few comments that Branislav Ivanovic made on the eve of the game, when he said that he would stop me by kicking me. I read those remarks and thought, All the best, pal. You've got to catch me to kick me.

I'd have quite enjoyed a 50-50 with Ivanovic, but instead ended up nose to nose with Diego Costa after I rattled him with a challenge that he didn't like. Costa rolled around, holding his ankle as if he'd been shot, and then he jumped up, thinking I was going to back down when he put his face in mine. No chance.

I came in at half-time and said to Wes and Huthy, 'Get into him. He'll lose his head.' Costa is one of those players who looks like he could flip. I play with plenty of aggression, but I'd never let anyone get into my mind or intimidate me physically.

At the interval we were already ahead after I converted Riyad's cross, and our man of the moment made it 2–0 in the second half with a sensational goal. Riyad turned César Azpilicueta inside out three or four times before bending a shot in the top corner. We won 2–1 and it turned out to be Jose Mourinho's last match as Chelsea manager. This time he wasn't paying me compliments in the corridor.

When we followed that up with a 3–2 win at Everton on the Saturday to guarantee top spot on Christmas Day, it was pointed out that in five of the previous six seasons the team that was top at Christmas had gone on to win the league. But we weren't taking too much notice of that kind of thing. Nobody said a word about the title in the dressing room. Claudio's message privately was the same as the one he gave publicly: 'It's all about getting to 40 points, forget anything else.'

The manager did, however, appreciate our efforts, and he was getting into the spirit of things. He gathered us together in the meeting room at the training ground before Christmas and said that he'd bought us a present each. All of the players and the staff were given a bell, engraved with Claudio's name on it, which a few of us thought a bit strange at first, and then the penny dropped that it was all about his 'Dilly-ding, dilly-dong' catchphrase. What a brilliant touch.

The next two fixtures were difficult on paper and didn't bring much festive cheer. We lost 1–0 at Liverpool on Boxing Day in a match that I should have missed. I had a bug and spent the morning of the game in the steam room at the hotel trying – and failing – to sweat it out. And then we drew 0–0 with Manchester City at the King Power Stadium, where I wore blacked-out boots because I was having a dispute with Nike over a new deal.

Nike were basically saying that because I didn't play for one of the 'big clubs', I didn't deserve to be on any more money, even though their boots were plastered over every newspaper for weeks because of the goalscoring record, we were top of the table and I was now an England international.

For a long time I was on Nike's 'share-of-pitch' deal, which was worth £1,000 a goal and £1,000 a game. It was a fraction of what plenty of other players were earning, especially at what Nike call their Category A clubs. My agent was annoyed, especially as we had a letter from Nike promising to renegotiate if I got an England call-up. Eventually, it got resolved but, like everything in my career, it felt like we had to fight for every penny.

• • •

Come the turn of the year, there was a risk that I wasn't going to be wearing any boots at all for a while because my groin was causing me big problems. I'd hardly trained since the Watford game back in November, relying on anaesthetic jabs to get me through matches. After talking things through with Dave Rennie, we decided to get back in touch with David Lloyd, the consultant surgeon I'd seen during the goalscoring run. David had developed something called the 'Lloyd release procedure', which was done through keyhole surgery and, crucially, he promised that it would have me back playing within two weeks.

I played in the goalless draw against Bournemouth on 2 January, and then we took the view that, with the FA Cup third round coming up, it was the best opportunity to get the operation done. I was happy to do it if it meant I would be pain-free for the rest of the season.

The procedure involved releasing the inguinal ligament on both groins by making a little cut in it to pull it away from the pubic bone, to ease the tension around where I was getting the discomfort, and then he puts in a mesh to give support to the groin area.

I had the operation less than 24 hours after the Bournemouth game, and when I woke up Dave Rennie told me that the tear in the ligament I'd had the cortisone injection in was huge. Although I stayed overnight at Nuffield Hospital in Leicester, I went straight into the training ground the next day to do some movement work to make sure that it didn't stiffen up.

We'd hit the 40-point target in the Bournemouth match, so every game was seen as a free one after that, and it was strange to recall the conversations we'd had among ourselves at the start of the season, when we looked through the fixture list and highlighted the tricky periods. In our eyes, Christmas looked awful, and we needed to be safe before we played the final three games, against Manchester United, Everton and Chelsea, because that was an atrocious run of matches to finish the season. Yet with 18 games of the season remaining the threat of relegation had gone, so the pressure was off and we could enjoy ourselves, starting with the visit to White Hart Lane on 13 January.

It was only ten days after I'd undergone surgery, and I made the starting lineup. It seemed incredible, really. I lasted 71 minutes and felt good, but I felt even better when I watched Huthy wind his neck back and head one into the top corner late on to give us a 1–0 win. On Twitter after the game he posted: 'It's not often that having a square-shaped head comes in useful', which was classic Huthy.

He went down a storm on social media again the following game, when we beat Stoke 3–0 and he fancied a go at putting a free-kick in the top corner. After some miscommunication, he almost collided with Drinky, and he shanked the ball out for a throw-in. 'Nine times out of ten they creep in the top corner … honestly', he posted on Twitter later.

I scored my first goal in seven matches in that Stoke game – the problem with my groin was definitely affecting the runs I was making prior to the surgery – and by the time we played next, against Liverpool on 2 February, I'd agreed to sign a new contract. There was some talk in January that a few clubs were interested in signing me, but I always wanted to stay. My agent had been keeping me up to speed with the negotiations but we'd reached a bit of an impasse, so Vichai, the owner, got involved and asked me to see him at the stadium.

He's got a private function room – I'd never been in there before – and we had a chat about my situation. I understood that the club needed to stay within the financial fair play framework, so I wasn't ignoring that side of things, and Vichai talked about how valuable I was to Leicester, making it clear that he didn't want to lose me. In the end I got a pay rise on the contract I signed back in August 2014, but the terms weren't as good as my agent had hoped to secure now that I was an England international, so the club agreed to insert a £22 million release clause as a compromise.

The next three games looked huge: Liverpool at home, Manchester City and Arsenal away. Adrian Butchart, the screenwriter who had decided to make a film about my life story on the back of my record-breaking goal against Manchester United, came to see me play in the flesh for the first time in the Liverpool match. I had a brief chance to introduce myself beforehand, when he was being shown around the stadium and I bumped into him outside the dressing rooms.

A couple of hours later I introduced myself on the pitch with one of the best goals I've ever scored. I'd seen Simon Mignolet, the Liverpool keeper, off his line a lot in the first half and he wasn't really retreating that quickly. When I walked out with Riyad for the second half I said to him, 'If you're near the halfway line and you touch it inside, shoot, because he's standing that far out.'

So that was in my mind as soon as Riyad played the ball over the top for me to run on to in the right-hand channel, and I had a little glance. I saw that Mignolet was not far off the edge of the box when the ball first bounced, so I was always going to hit it straight away – and thank God I did. From 27 yards out the ball exploded off my right boot and flew past Mignolet. The King Power Stadium was a cauldron of noise and there was absolute mayhem in the stands. I ran towards the corner flag with no idea how to celebrate because I couldn't quite believe what had just happened. I don't score many like that, and if you look at my face as Danny Simpson runs over to congratulate me, it's an expression that basically says, What the hell have I just done?

We ended up winning 2–0 against Liverpool and I also got the second, my 18th Premier League goal of the season, to cap a perfect night. Claudio must have had a drink after the game because he was trying to compare my goal to Marco van Basten's volley for Holland in the 1988 European Championship. Even Jürgen Klopp, Liverpool's manager, seemed quietly impressed. 'It's nice to be in a stadium where Jamie Vardy scored goal of the month, but in an ideal world not when you're manager of the other team,' he said.

• • •

The day after the game I met up with Adrian to talk about the film. I just couldn't get my head around the idea when my agent first told me that a screenwriter in Los Angeles wanted to make a Hollywood movie about me. And why would it make sense to me? I just see myself as a lad from Sheffield who's scored a few goals.

There'd even been talk in the papers about who would play me in the film – people like Zac Efron and Louis Tomlinson were mentioned – and, to be honest, it felt like the world had gone bonkers. But after chatting with Adrian at Stapleford Park, a country hotel not far from our home in Melton Mowbray, both Becky and I could see that he was really serious about the film, especially when he told us that he was going on a night out with the Inbetweeners as part of his research.

Yet it wasn't just my story that was capturing the imagination. Football fans everywhere were fascinated by what Leicester were doing. When I looked at social media it felt as though everybody was willing us on, saying how pleased they were that a so-called smaller club was not afraid to go up against the big boys and give them a bloody nose. And that's the mentality we had in the dressing room. We were just going out and enjoying ourselves and, to put it bluntly, not giving a fuck who we were up against.

That showed at the Etihad Stadium four days after the Liverpool win. We went to Manchester City, one of the biggest clubs in the Premier League, and turned them over. We left the stadium feeling ten foot tall and, while we never shouted about it at the time, there was a clear sense from that moment that the team could do something special. Everything we did against City was spot on. They couldn't cope with our counter-attacks, Riyad was unplayable and Huthy got another two goals. What a feeling it was, looking up at the Leicester fans, stretched across three tiers, going mental.

The only downside for me was that I was drug tested after the match, which was a pain in the arse because I needed to get away from the stadium quickly for an engagement party. The problem with having your urine tested after a game is that you often don't need a piss. I remember sitting in the testing room with Marc Albrighton (Sharky) and Shinji, thinking this could take a while, so I asked for some beers to try to speed up the process. Manchester City's Raheem Sterling, Fabian Delph and Yaya Touré were in there with us, and they politely declined my offer of a drink when the bottles arrived, so Shinji, Sharky and I toasted our victory while waiting to give a sample. I think I was seven down by the time I delivered.

I had an interesting experience with a drug tester earlier that season, when someone turned up unannounced at our home at nine o'clock at night. We heard the buzzer go and thought it was another prankster, because we were getting a lot of hoax calls around that time, but the voice at the other end said that they were from doping control and they had come to carry out a random drug test.

Fair enough, but the problem, once again, was that I didn't need a piss. After chatting for a bit, I said I'd go and get a beer from the bar. I think one of the guys thought I meant a local pub, but before he got his coat I explained that I had a bar in the house. I decided to get on the Kopparberg and, thinking that it could be a while before nature called, turned on the PlayStation.

After more than two hours of watching me drink cider and play *Call of Duty*, the drug testers finally had their sample. I can still remember them leaving at 11:30pm, because a long night ended with one of them, for reasons I couldn't fathom, deciding against reversing up the drive and going into the neighbour's to whip the car around. Instead, he attempted to execute a U-turn where there wasn't enough space, and as he went back and forth about 37 times it was like watching Austin Powers getting his luggage truck stuck in Dr Evil's headquarters. Still, they had what they wanted, and I'd managed to get a couple of hours in on *Call of Duty*, so everybody was happy.

• • •

Claudio got us all together for our usual debrief after the 3–1 win at Manchester City. It was important analysis that everybody always took seriously, yet Claudio also had this wonderful ability to inject a bit of humour into proceedings. It not only lightened the mood, it gave you the feeling that the staff and players were on the same page – working hard but having fun at the same time.

Riyad scored a great goal at City but it wasn't the best celebration, because he got his knee caught in the turf when he tried to slide in front of our fans and he could have badly injured himself. So Claudio showed the clip of Riyad scoring and tumbling over afterwards and, with no hint of what was to come, said, 'Stop, stop. Riyad, you love this celebration?'

Riyad said, 'No, no.'

Claudio said, 'Are you sure?'

We were all looking a little confused, most of all Riyad. Then Claudio got Andy Blake, one of the performance analysts, to show another clip, and up came some footage of Riyad scoring for Algeria on what looked like the driest pitch in the world. He did exactly the same celebration as against Manchester City, and the whole room broke into laughter.

Something similar happened after the Newcastle game at St James' Park, back in November, when Shinji scored such a funny goal. He jumped up for a header inside the six-yard box, mistimed his leap, the ball bounced back up off the floor, hit him on the forehead and went in. Watching that back in the meeting room, everybody was laughing not just at the goal, but at Shinji's reaction. He was celebrating with the biggest grin ever on his face.

We then had a date with Arsenal on Valentine's Day. It was a big game, even if we were shunning all the title-race hype, and on the stroke of half-time we were awarded a penalty after Nacho Monreal brought me down. I put the ball on the spot and, as I waited for the referee's whistle, Olivier Giroud walked past me and said, 'You're going to shit it.' I smashed the ball past Petr Cech and went straight to Giroud. 'Who's going to shit it?' I said to him.

To be fair to Giroud, I don't mind that kind of thing. It's part and parcel of the game and I'd do it to an opponent if I thought it would get us an advantage. But the truth is that he only made me more determined to score.

Unfortunately, we lost Danny Simpson to a second yellow card early in the second half, and when Theo Walcott equalised with 20 minutes to go it was backs-to-the-wall time. We were hanging on – N'Golo was unbelievable that day, almost a freak of nature with the amount of running he did – but in the fifth minute of injury time Danny Welbeck scored. We were devastated – absolutely gutted. It was such a kick in the teeth to battle that hard and come away with nothing.

In the dressing room afterwards Simmo held his hand up straight away and said sorry for getting sent off. We all said that he had nothing to apologise for. Signed from QPR at the start of the previous season, Simmo had been superb since coming into the side around October time, and he totally bought into the team ethic. In any case, we'd never single a player out. We were in it together. We won as a team, and we lost as a team. That's what made us such a tight group.

The defeat was a blow, of course, and it was one of those results that you can't wait to get out of the system. Unfortunately, we didn't have a game for another 13 days because it was the FA Cup the following weekend and we'd already been knocked out, so it promised to be a long couple of weeks.

What followed was a fantastic piece of management from Claudio. He pulled Wes aside for a quiet word and then said to us all, 'You played brilliantly. I can't fault you for what you've done today. You've fought right until the end and I'm absolutely gutted for you. I've just had a word with the captain and you can all have a week off.'

We'd expected to be in at the training ground until Wednesday, but now we could all have a proper break, forget about Arsenal and come back re-energised. I went to Dubai with Becky and the kids, and Jeff Schlupp, Simmo, Huthy, Liam Moore, Drinky and Matty James were out there as well with their partners and families. Instead of being at the training ground together, it was like a Leicester City holiday camp.

The Sunderland team were also in Dubai and staying at the same hotel, but they must have booked with another tour operator, because they had a different schedule to us. I would watch them running up and down the beach while I took a sip from my bottle of Corona, before dropping the sun lounger back a couple of notches and closing my eyes. I was already feeling better.

* * *

We returned for training the following week with the result at the Emirates out of our minds. We were determined to respond in exactly the same way as we had earlier in the season when we lost the first time against Arsenal. Norwich had been our opponents back then and they were also lying in wait on 27 February. It looked like being a frustrating afternoon, but Leo came off the bench to get an 89th minute winner after I just about got my studs to Sharky's cross.

By the time we took on Newcastle at home, on 14 March, we'd picked up another four points, against West Brom and Watford, and were still top with nine games remaining. Claudio was not entertaining title talk, but he wasn't tolerating second-rate performances either. Half-time against Newcastle was the only time I saw him properly lose it with us. Shinji scored a brilliant overhead kick to give us the lead – the most infectious smile in football was beaming again – but Newcastle had parked the bus, in what was Rafael Benítez's first game in charge, and we were struggling to move it. Claudio was upset with what he was seeing. He didn't think it was the Leicester he'd come to know, which, in fairness, we'd already said to each other in our players' half-time chat.

The player discussion may come as a surprise to some people, but it happened every game. At half-time Claudio always walked straight past where we were sitting to have a chat with a few of the staff, leaving the players to talk between ourselves about what we thought was going right and wrong. After a few minutes Claudio would come to speak to us, and if we were still going over things he'd let us carry on, listen to what we were saying and then give his views.

When you've got strong characters in your dressing room and players who respect one another, you can do that kind of thing, because it doesn't descend into slagging each other off. We have the player discussions because we care about the team, not just our own individual performance, and a lot of the lads say their piece, especially the senior members such as Wes, Kasper, Huthy, Christian Fuchs, Drinky and me.

We held on for victory against Newcastle, which was all that mattered at that stage of the season, to go five points clear of Tottenham. When we won at Crystal Palace five days later it was pretty clear what the fans thought about the way the title race was shaping up. One of our media lads came into the dressing room at Selhurst Park half an hour after the game and said, 'The fans are still here. They're not leaving.'

I got up and went to have a peek around the tunnel, and there they were, thousands of them, singing their hearts out. 'We're going to win the league' was ringing out again and again. It was extraordinary. It really struck a chord with me, because I've been a fan and I know what it's like travelling all over the country, standing up all game, cheering your team on and hoping that you'll get acknowledged by the players at the final whistle. Those Leicester supporters – who had to be politely asked to leave by the stadium announcer in the end – were having the time of their lives, really believing that the unthinkable could happen. Maybe the same thought was starting to go through our minds in the dressing room, too.

• • •

Two days before the Palace game there was a nice moment at the training ground when Dave, the physio, came out to break some news. N'Golo had been called up to the France squad for the first time and Drinky was in the England squad. Training stopped as everyone congratulated the boys, shaking hands and high-fiving.

'God, N'Golo. I'm honoured,' Drinky said. 'I'm playing with a France international.'

'Hang on a minute, Drinky,' I said. 'N'Golo's playing with an England international.'

Drinky just looked at me. 'Yeah, you!' he replied, clearly not thinking of himself as an England player just yet.

Later that day I had to get to Wembley for the launch of Nike's new England kit. I didn't really fancy sitting in the car all afternoon in rush-hour traffic in and out of London, so I thought I'd see if Vichai and Top would let me hitch a ride in their helicopter. I asked Puchong Masayavanij, the assistant club secretary, who is from Thailand and regularly speaks to the owner, to see if there was any possibility of getting on board the helicopter. To my surprise and delight, I was told it was fine. So we took off from the training ground – just the two pilots, with me in the back – and landed at an RAF base in London, not far from Wembley, about 40 minutes later.

As well as modelling the England kit, there were a few interviews to do, some with a view to the friendly against Germany on Saturday week. I was given some questions in advance to prepare, and one of them was whether I had any memories of England v Germany games. I mentioned to John, my agent, about the pint being thrown at the TV in the Old Blue Ball pub after Lampard's goal wasn't given in the 2010 World Cup, but we both agreed that it probably wasn't the sort of answer they were looking for.

The friendly in Berlin turned out to be one of the greatest days of my career. I received a few messages on the eve of the game, pointing out that Joachim Löw, the Germany coach, had described me as a 'spectacular player' and said that they'd been studying ways of stopping me. It was a terrific thing to hear, but I was just desperate for my first England goal.

With 19 minutes to go against Germany, and not long after Harry Kane had scored a superb goal to get us back into the game, I came on for Danny Welbeck. Three minutes later, Nathaniel Clyne, who's got pace to burn, got beyond the full-back and, just as he was about to cross, I made a darting run across the front of centre-half Antonio Rüdiger. The ball was just behind me, so the only thing I could do was flick it with my heel on the half-volley. I could not have connected any sweeter, and the ball flashed inside Manuel Neuer's near post.

Get in! I'd finally done it. My first goal for my country, against Germany, the World Cup winners no less, and with Neuer in goal – that takes some topping. The celebration was quite restrained in the circumstances – I think I was in a state of shock. I puffed my cheeks out, put one arm in the air and ran to Clyney, before disappearing in a sea of red shirts. It was a sensational feeling, totally different to the record-breaking goal against Manchester United, when everything was unhinged. With the goal against Germany I felt a sense of pride more than anything, though I still hadn't come to terms with what had happened after the final whistle, when I looked through all the messages on my phone and just sent a simple text to my agent that said: 'What just happened there?'

A photograph emerged after the Germany game showing Harry Kane alongside me on the bench at Vicarage Road for the play-off semi-final second-leg defeat against Watford in 2013. Neither of us could get in the Leicester team at the time and nor could Drinky, who was also pictured among the substitutes. Less than three years later we were all in the England squad – it's crazy how things can change in football.

I didn't have to wait long for my second England goal, which arrived three days later in a 2–1 defeat against Holland. Ruud van Nistelrooy was Holland's assistant manager, and it was a really nice gesture on his part to come into the England dressing room to personally congratulate me on breaking his Premier League goalscoring record.

The England kit man said to me after the game that Schalke striker Klaas-Jan Huntelaar had asked for my shirt, so I happily handed it over. Bastian Schweinsteiger had requested my jersey after the Germany game, and Wazza was on TV on the night of the Holland match saying that his son wanted an England shirt with 'Vardy' on the back. Life was becoming more and more surreal.

While it was nice to get another England goal, especially as it was my first at Wembley, I was most pleased for Drinky, whose first England appearance ended with him being named man of the match. We spoke to the media together in the lead-up to the Germany game and I called him the 'puppet master', which is exactly what he is because he pulls all the strings in midfield.

I hoped that my two England goals would give me a bit of momentum in the Premier League because I hadn't scored since converting a penalty at Arsenal, but it was Wes who got the winner in a 1–0 victory over Southampton. The game fell on the eve of Vichai's birthday, so the owner treated all the fans to a free beer and a doughnut. We sang happy birthday to him in the dressing room, and the three points seemed like the best possible present for him. With Spurs drawing at Liverpool 24 hours earlier, we were now seven points clear at the top with only six games left. The Premier League title was the subject everyone was thinking about but didn't dare to mention.

It was Christian Fuchs's 30th birthday in the week, and his wife, Raluca, who lives in New York, had organised a surprise bash at a restaurant in Leicester. What none of the players realised until the night of the party was that Claudio had got the dates mixed up and gone to the same venue 24 hours earlier, only to walk into an empty room. Jon Sanders, the player liaison officer, got the blame, although it was almost certainly Claudio's fault. But how many Premier League managers would go to one of their player's birthday parties once, let alone twice? Not only that, but he was happy to do a little speech in front of everyone when Christian asked him to explain what had happened.

While the mood around the club was jovial and relaxed, I had a bad day at the office in the lead-up to the Sunderland game the following Sunday when I ended up walking off the training pitch. We were playing a round-robin five-a-side tournament on the Wednesday morning and nothing was going right for me. I felt that I was letting the team down and I'd had enough. I needed my own space so I went off into the gym and got on the treadmill before doing a bike session. I knew it wasn't the right thing to do, so when I calmed down I stopped Claudio when he was walking towards his office and asked him for a chat.

'Are you OK?' he said.

'I'm fine. I was just shit in training,' I replied. 'I thought it was best for me to remove myself from the situation.'

'I understand, but you can't just walk off,' Claudio said. 'If you walk off, the first thing I think is that you are injured.'

'No, I was just having a bad session and my head had gone. I'm sorry,' I said.

Claudio understood and didn't make a big deal about it. But he told me that in future I should go and talk to him if I ever felt like that again, and he'd then send me inside so that it looks more professional than me throwing my toys out of the pram. In fairness, it was a one-off, and I knew I'd never do it again.

Later that week I was throwing socks rather than toys, and it proved to be a good omen. We'd often play a little game at the training ground where we'd roll up a sock, put it in the bath to get it wet and heavy, and then launch it at someone. On the Saturday morning Christian Fuchs was watching me out the corner of his eye as he was getting changed, thinking I was going to target him. I said, 'No, don't worry. I'm going to throw it in the bin from here, and when it goes in I'm going to score tomorrow.' It was a tiny target on the other side of the room, but the sock sailed in.

With a wet sock and a glass of port on my side, I didn't think I could go wrong against Sunderland, but the first half at the Stadium of Light didn't go to plan. I was making all my normal runs but a few of the passes were going a bit astray, so I started to get agitated. Shit, this is not going to be our day, I thought.

Perhaps Claudio had arrived at the same conclusion, because at half-time he came over and spoke to me in a way that made me feel that I couldn't let him down. 'Come on, Jamie. I need something from you,' he said.

Midway through the second half it clicked. Drinky, with his fifth assist of the season for me, delivered a perfectly weighted through ball that encouraged me to run in behind Younès Kaboul. Once I touched the ball there was only one place I could put my shot, so I opened up my body and, in my best impression of Thierry Henry, slotted it into the far corner. I was right back on my game and, with Sunderland pushing for an equaliser, I found myself through on goal again in injury time. Demarai Gray, who'd joined from Birmingham in January, brought the ball down with a lovely piece of control and found me on the halfway line. I was one-on-one with left-back Patrick van Aanholt and just bulldozed my way past him, rounded Vito Mannone, the Sunderland keeper, and for a split-second thought about blasting the ball as hard as I could into the empty net. Instead, I tapped in my 21st Premier League goal of the season. It was game over, and at the other end of the stadium the Leicester fans were toasting another victory that edged us closer to the title.

There was talk afterwards about me becoming the first Leicester player to score more than 20 top-flight goals in a season since Gary Lineker in 1984–85, but I genuinely felt that the focus deserved to be on the lads at the other end of the pitch every bit as much as me. That was our fifth successive clean sheet, and our back four – Simmo, Wes, Huthy and Christian – plus Kasper were the unsung heroes.

Claudio was emotional at the final whistle, which I didn't realise until later because I was busy chatting to a little lad who ran onto the pitch and asked for my shirt. He reminded me of myself when I was a kid, but unfortunately I'd already promised my shirt to someone else. 'Well, can I have a hug then?' he said. So I gave him one and then, with the benefit of experience said, 'Go on, get yourself off before you get into trouble.'

With Spurs winning later in the day, our lead at the top remained seven points, but it was a plane full of happy players that touched down at East Midlands airport later that day. I was standing on the bus taking us back to the terminal when Claudio called me over. He showed me a text and explained that it was from Carlo Verdone, a famous Italian actor, screenwriter and director. The message said: 'Can you tell Jamie Vardy that everyone in Rome loves him, he is the Caesar of Leicester.' So Claudio gave me his phone to reply. I typed in: 'Thank you. But I'm not Caesar. The whole team is Caesar.' I handed Claudio his phone. He read the message and just nodded his head.

13

CHAMPIONS!

I barged open the dressing-room door, threw my shirt down and turned on the TV. I was *raging*. I couldn't sit down. There was a chair in front of me and I held onto the back of it, gripping it so tightly that my knuckles turned white.

As the TV came to life, I watched a replay of the sending off, from a camera at the opposite end of the ground. Jon Moss, the referee, was 40 yards away, without a clear view, yet he decided that I dived. Not only that, but he couldn't wait to get his cards out. There was no thinking time.

I heard the door open and assumed it was one of the staff, but Becky walked in. She was worried that I'd lose it and start rearranging the dressing room, and her instincts weren't far off, the way I was feeling. It was the first time I'd been sent off as a professional footballer and, with only four matches remaining and the Premier League title in sight, the timing could not have been worse.

Not that I was thinking that far ahead. A sense of injustice was burning inside me as I looked at my teammates running their bollocks off, trying to protect our 1–0 lead against West Ham. There was still more than half an hour remaining.

It looked like we would hold on, but with six minutes to go Moss decided that he wanted a bit more of the action. He penalised Wes for fouling Winston Reid in the area. Wes had his hands on Reid, granted, but the West Ham defender made a lot of it and flung himself to the floor. Andy Carroll equalised from the spot, cancelling out the goal I'd scored in the first half, and two minutes later Aaron Cresswell made it 2–1 with a tremendous left-foot shot. As the ball arced over Kasper's head and into the top corner I held my head in my hands. I felt angry and helpless. I wanted to chase a lost cause, make another run, force a mistake, throw myself at a cross. Yet all I could do was stand and watch.

With the game deep into injury time, Becky headed back upstairs, leaving me alone in my thoughts. I knew that if we lost it would be seen by others as the moment when Leicester finally cracked. Yet I still hadn't given up on the game, not with the spirit and fight in that group of players on the pitch. We'd proved time and again that we never knew when we were beaten, rescuing points from desperate situations, and even with ten men I thought we'd get another chance.

What I didn't realise was that Moss had another controversial decision in him. After turning down our appeals for a stonewall penalty after Angelo Ogbonna had his arm around Huthy's neck – the West Ham centre-half did the same thing to me in the first half – the referee penalised Carroll for a foul on Jeff that was the softest call of the lot. It felt like a classic case of a referee deciding that two wrongs make a right. Not that I was complaining at this stage, of course. Leo, showing balls of steel, slotted home, and I jumped around in the dressing room like the Leicester fans I could hear behind the goal.

Suddenly, it seemed like a point gained, and the mood among the lads when they got back into the dressing room was one of defiance. They were furious with the referee, who'd looked like a man in charge of a game that was too big for him, but the way we salvaged a draw gave everybody something positive to focus on.

At home that evening I was thinking back over everything. Not just the red card, but the implications of it – I was going to be suspended for the visit of Swansea the following Sunday, and that made me feel like I'd let the lads down. I was missing at the critical stage of the season. I grabbed my phone and posted a message on the players' WhatsApp group: 'Sorry, boys. I'm gutted I won't be able to fight with you next week.'

The responses came thick and fast. Everybody was telling me that there was no need to apologise and, in a sign that the West Ham match had strengthened, not weakened our resolve, promised to hammer Swansea next week.

But it soon became clear that Swansea might not be the only game that I would have to sit out. The way I reacted to my red card had turned into a big talking point. There were pictures showing me jabbing a finger in the direction of Moss, plus a suggestion that I swore at him. All of which led to talk that the mandatory one-match suspension could be extended to two games, which would mean that I'd also be banned for the trip to Old Trafford the week after Swansea.

I honestly couldn't remember what I said to Moss when I was first asked about it by the club. All I knew was that I was furious and I wouldn't have called him a cheat – that's the worst thing you can say to a referee. But once I watched the replays I didn't need to be a professional lip-reader to work it out: 'That's a fucking shambles, you fucking cunt.'

It doesn't make for good viewing, let alone good reading. I know children are watching and that we're supposed to be role models, so I don't just let that kind of thing wash over me. I wish I'd responded in a different way, but sometimes it's uncontrollable out on the pitch. Unless you've been in that situation, in the heat of the moment, it's hard to understand the emotions that you go through, because everything happens so quickly. One second you're fine and the next your blood's boiling. It's unrealistic to think that you can slow everything down and consider carefully what you're saying or how you react, especially when you feel that you're on the wrong end of a bad decision that has severe consequences for you and your team. And that's exactly how I felt in the West Ham match. In my eyes I'd been unfairly penalised.

When I heard the whistle, my first thought was that Moss had given a penalty. Then he put his arm the other way and went to his pocket. People can say what they want about that decision – and opinion was divided at the time – but I'll argue all day long that I did not dive. I'd love to see anyone who can sprint like me and stay on their feet when they're pulled or nudged. It's impossible. I've seen the replays from every angle. Ogbonna pulls me back at first. Then, as a striker you're taught from when you first start learning the game to put your body between the defender and the ball. As I've done that my right leg has got trapped in between both of his, while he's running. It's just a tangle of legs – not a penalty or a dive.

A similar thing happened between Dan Gosling and me when we played Bournemouth at home on 2 January. The referee that day was Andre Marriner – one of the top two officials in my opinion, along with Mark Clattenburg, because they're not arrogant and they talk to you. Marriner gave a goal kick, which was the correct decision.

But it wasn't just the second yellow card Moss showed me that pissed me off. The foul he penalised me for in the first half on Cheikhou Kouyaté was never a booking. I slid in to make a challenge but it was at the side of Kouyaté, and the West Ham midfielder then unintentionally left a four-inch stud mark along the top of my thigh as he tried to skip over me. People were saying the next day that Moss had warned me for previous tackles when he handed out my first yellow card, but that was nonsense.

Even a couple of the West Ham lads were supportive when I got sent off. Mark Noble, the West Ham captain, came over and put an arm around me and said that he didn't think I deserved to go. Then Michail Antonio, another West Ham player, said, 'Just walk off. Don't get yourself into any more shit.'

But the damage had already been done. On Monday came the predictable news that I'd been charged by the Football Association with improper conduct. To compound things, Spurs won 4–0 at Stoke that night with a performance that seemed to have most people outside of Leicester thinking Harry Kane had it right when he'd posted a picture on Instagram of four lions about to hunt down their prey after our draw with West Ham.

It was going to be a long week. Not because I was worried about Spurs catching us, but because I had no game at the weekend to focus on and I knew that it would kill me to be in the stands watching my mates. I'd started 45 Premier League games on the spin, playing across that period with broken bones in my wrist, pain-killing injections in my groin and my foot, and I even managed to squeeze in an operation. Yet now I was out, and no matter how much I wanted to get on the pitch, how long I spent in the cryotherapy chamber singing ballads, or how much I pleaded with Dave Rennie to load the needle with some anaesthetic, it wouldn't make a blind bit of difference.

• • •

The fall-out from the West Ham game filled plenty of column inches in the papers that week, and I received a lot of messages of support, including a public one from Roy Hodgson, which I really appreciated.

But by Thursday, we knew that there wasn't much option other than to accept the FA's improper conduct charge. The only avenue open to me was to plead guilty and request a personal hearing to explain why I reacted like I did. We agreed to go down that route and drew a line under the episode for a few days, until the Monday when the hearing was scheduled, so everybody at Leicester could focus solely on the Swansea match.

A lot of people in the media took the view that my absence would significantly weaken the team, but I've got no idea why. Leicester's success up until that point had been built around the group, and that showed against Swansea. Leo, ever reliable whenever called upon, started up front in place of me and scored twice, and when Sharky came off the bench to add a fourth late on, our fans were singing 'four–nil to the one-man team'. That made me smile.

We were now within five points of winning the Premier League title, but there was no time to rest. Straight after the match we all had to dash to the Grosvenor House Hotel in London for the Professional Footballers' Association awards dinner. With our game not finishing until just before 6pm, time was against us, so helicopters took us from Leicester to London, and we had a bit of fun on the way.

I was in a helicopter with Claudio, Drinky, Kasper and one of the directors. We were flying above west London when Claudio looked out the window and pointed to where he lives.

'It's over there, near the park,' he said, prompting us all to lean to the side and gaze out.

'You know what that smells of, don't you, boss?' I said.

'What?' said Claudio, with a confused expression.

'Cash,' I replied.

He just looked at me and chuckled.

It turned into that sort of evening – relaxed and plenty of laughs over a few beers, as well as lots of recognition for the lads. Four Leicester players were named in the PFA team of the year – me, Riyad, N'Golo and Wes – but it could easily have been more. John Terry posted a picture showing that he'd picked seven of us in the side he selected, and that spoke volumes.

Riyad was named Players' Player of the Year, which was thoroughly deserved, and I picked up a special award from Gordon Taylor, the PFA chief executive, for becoming the first player to score in 11 successive Premier League matches. I made a point on stage of thanking Riyad for being dragged off against Bournemouth, because I'd never have taken the penalty that started the goalscoring run if he'd been on the pitch.

• • •

The following day I had my personal hearing at Wembley. It was a three-man panel, chaired by Stuart Ripley, the former Blackburn Rovers winger. They told me that I hadn't been charged for anything I'd said to the referee, and instead explained that it was all about my reaction, pointing at Moss and not leaving the field straight away.

Jon Rudkin, Leicester's director of football, was with me at the hearing. We said our piece, and we were asked to return in 10 minutes for the verdict. They gave me the additional one-game ban, said that I was being fined £10,000 and I had to pay £500 towards the cost of the hearing itself. And just to rub a bit of salt into my wounds at the end of what felt like a totally pointless exercise, they said, 'Thank you for coming. We thought you handled yourself really well.'

It meant another week on the sidelines for me, and the significance of that would become clear later in the day, when Tottenham played West Brom at White Hart Lane. I decided against sitting down and watching it, as I just wanted to focus on what I could control, preferring instead to play *Call of Duty* on the PlayStation with the game on in the background. Becky was following the match much more closely, and getting overly worked up about it.

'I can't watch this – I'm too nervous,' she said.

'Relax, don't worry. It's all down to us,' I replied, concentrating on *Call of Duty*.

And that was genuinely how I felt. I couldn't see any reason why we wouldn't be capable of getting the points we needed, irrespective of Tottenham's results, to win the league.

Spurs took the lead against West Brom in the first half through a Craig Dawson own goal, which encouraged us both to have an early night and catch up on some sleep after staying in London for the PFA awards. I put the TV on in bed, just to see if anything had changed, and Becky nodded off. All of a sudden, Dawson equalised. I couldn't believe it.

'Fucking hell, West Brom have scored!' I said, waking Becky up in the process.

Spurs couldn't find a winning goal and dropped two points, which felt like a huge shift because we were now within one match of being crowned Premier League champions. That was the good news. The bad news was that on the back of the personal hearing earlier in the day, I wasn't going to be on the pitch at Old Trafford to play a part in trying to get us over the line.

The suspension was painful, and with no game to prepare for until the penultimate weekend of the season, I threw everything into training. So much so that Claudio pulled me aside after one session.

'Last week and this week, you trained very hard. Why do you not do this all the time?' he said.

'I need to save my legs, boss, and make sure they're 100 per cent for games,' I replied.

'That's all in your mind,' Claudio said.

'No, that's me knowing, from past experience, exactly what I need to do to make sure that I'm fit,' I explained.

Claudio just had a little smile.

If I trained every single day as I played, come match day I would blow up, because I wouldn't have anything left in me. I consciously hold a bit back on the training ground, making sure that I'm ready to go at it hammer and tongs when the game comes along.

At Old Trafford I sat in the directors' box next to Matty James, who was continuing his rehabilitation from the knee injury he suffered a year ago. We didn't know what the protocol was if your team scored – was it the done thing to celebrate? – but we were both on our feet when Wes popped up with another crucial header to equalise. A 1–1 draw meant that we still needed two points to win the league, unless Spurs failed to beat Chelsea the following evening, in which case the title would be ours.

In the dressing room at Old Trafford I suggested watching the Spurs game at my place. We had plenty of space there and most people had been round before, for the party we hosted 14 months ago, when we were bottom of the league and in need of a pick-me-up. How times had changed.

Everyone seemed happy with that idea, although we agreed that it was best to keep it quiet, as we didn't want to alert the media or make it look like we were counting our chickens.

Bank Holiday Monday got off to a good start when the Football Writers' Association announced that I'd been named their Footballer of the Year. I got wind of the news on Saturday night and was delighted to hear that I was going to be picking up such a prestigious award later in the week. And the day was about to get even better.

• • •

Seven hours and a lot of Stella-numbed pain later, the latest tattoo to add to my collection was well underway across my back, hips and stomach. The design was of a pocket watch, carrying Sofia's time and date of birth, cupped in a hand with roses around it. I already had four tattoos, including 'Carpe Diem' across my back – 'Seize the day' sums up my attitude to life.

Christian Fuchs and Huthy swung by to pick me up to head to my place for the Spurs game, and as we turned the corner outside my house in Melton Mowbray I started to wonder whether I'd invited the whole of Leicester. The news that 'Jamie Vardy's having a party' had spread like wildfire. Fans, journalists, photographers and TV crews were camped outside, lining the road. The flashbulbs popped as we pulled into the drive, but I kept my head down in the back and somehow managed to get smuggled into my own party without anyone noticing.

Inside, we were in for a rollercoaster ride. Everyone was relaxed at first, but we soon had our Leicester-tinted lenses on as we kicked every ball, made every tackle and complained about every decision just like we were playing the match ourselves. A Spurs foul that warranted no more than a talking to was met with shouts of 'Defo a red card!', and the swear box got a top-up when Harry Kane put them ahead in the 35th minute. When Spurs went 2–0 up, the party felt like it was over – or at least postponed for another five days. Some of the boys tried to look on the bright side and reminded everyone that it was still in our hands – we'd just have to beat Everton at home on Saturday – yet there was no getting away from it: the evening had turned into an anti-climax.

And then it happened.

My England teammate Gary Cahill got Chelsea back into it with a goal – 'You fucking legend' was my reaction at the time, and the same three words were sent to him the next day. Now we had a game on our hands as both teams went for it.

It was the 83rd minute when that man Eden Hazard, who'd come on at half-time, picked up possession just inside his own half. He got away from Kyle Walker and slipped the ball into the feet of Diego Costa, who turned Toby Alderweireld and returned the pass to Hazard. It was a little under his feet and … unbelievable! He produced a piece of absolute magic, curling an incredible shot into the top corner. The room exploded into cheers and acrobatics as we went crazy, our celebrations every bit the equal of those on the pitch.

The match wasn't over yet, however, and when six minutes of injury time that seemed to go on for ever were up, it still carried on. But you couldn't see Spurs scoring another. Chelsea had broken them. Mark Clattenburg put the whistle to his mouth and then …

'Leicester City are champions of the Premier League,' Martin Tyler, the Sky commentator, said. 'The greatest story ever told has its happy ending for Claudio Ranieri and his players.'

Not that we could hear him above the roar of 'Championes! Championes! Olé! Olé! Olé!' Our house was shaking under the eruption of euphoria from a group of players who'd achieved the unthinkable. *We'd done it!* Never mind the greatest story ever told – this was the greatest feeling I'd ever known, being Premier League champions with a set of lads who'd do anything for one another.

We got the champagne out and I thought it was time to have a bit of fun on social media. I'd been biding my time ever since Harry Kane posted that picture of the lions about to go on a hunt. Not because I wanted to get my own back – I knew it was only friendly banter from Harry, who I get on well with. And my response was meant exactly the same way.

There's a time and a place to do things like that, and for me, that was the moment, rather than when nothing had been decided on the back of one result – which was what Arsenal did after beating us at the Emirates in February, when they posted selfies in the dressing room.

I'd had it in my mind for a while that I'd tweet a picture of a pack of hyenas if we won the title – and that was nothing to do with laughing. If you look up hyenas it says that they drive off larger predators, like lions, and they also hunt in packs. They're a team, whereas lions will often hunt alone. But then someone at Leicester sent me the picture of the *Lion King*'s

Mufasa falling down a cliff, and as soon as I saw it I thought, that's the one. I posted it straight away.

We could hear all the singing outside on the road, but there was a bit of a lull inside after the initial celebrations. It's hard to describe, but it was almost the calm after the storm, because everything fell really quiet, as if the reality of the situation had just hit home. One of the lads kept shaking his head in a state of disbelief, trying to take in the enormity of what had happened.

A few of the lads who had watched the game at home were now on their way to join us. Sharky drove over from Birmingham, Kasper came down from Manchester, and Ben Chilwell and Daniel Amartey dropped by, so everyone was there by the end of the night.

• • •

Later on, a few of the lads went out in town and booked themselves into hotels ahead of training the next day. I stayed at home and called it a day at 4:30am. I'm not sure what I was drinking come the end, but I spent a lot of time looking at that league table, with Leicester's name in gold, and wondering what on earth we'd gone and done.

Jon Sanders, the player liaison officer, picked me up for training the next morning. He said that he needed to collect a few of the lads from a hotel, and then he dropped the bombshell that I didn't have to be in until 10:30am because training had been put back an hour. I couldn't believe it – I had a hangover and I was going in an hour early. I'd have called in sick if I was working at the factory.

With none of the players in when I got to the training ground, I ended up going into the staff room. Walshy and Shakey were in there, along with a few others, and Claudio arrived about ten minutes later. He just looked at me when he walked through the door.

'You ever answer your phone?' he said.

I didn't know what he was talking about.

'I called you last night at the party,' he continued.

'Nah, you've not rang me,' I replied.

Then I looked at my phone and saw missed calls from a number I didn't recognise.

'Let me ring you now,' Claudio said.

And there it was, the same number that had been coming up on my phone when I was toasting the title. Little did I know, I'd been blanking the manager.

'Save it!' Claudio said, smiling.

It may seem strange to some people that I didn't have the manager's number in my phone but I could always speak to him at the training ground, and if we ever needed anything, or wanted to find out about times and venues, we'd always go through Jon Sanders.

Once all the players were in, Claudio called us together and asked us whether we wanted to keep to the schedule and train, which meant that we had the next day off, or swap things around so that we could have 24 hours off to recover from the night before. We all agreed that, as we'd come in, it made sense to do a session.

The rest of the staff then left the room and we were told to sit tight for a bit, before going to the gym, where everybody based at the training ground was waiting to give us a huge ovation. It was a really nice gesture, and Claudio and Wes both did a little speech afterwards.

Once training started, it felt like we spent more time posing for photos than running about – which was a good thing, given how we were all feeling. Vichai, the owner, wanted to take us all for lunch at San Carlo, a restaurant in Leicester, where huge crowds were waiting to greet us, but unfortunately I could only make a fleeting visit because I had a pre-arranged sponsor event for England in Manchester.

I was whisked off in a helicopter, looking a little dishevelled to say the least. Normally, I can't stand being in the makeup area, but it was definitely needed on that occasion. As soon as I arrived at the TV studio I said, 'Can you get rid of these bags, please?' Robbie Fowler was there that day, laughing at the state of me as well as asking what on earth I was doing turning up.

He said that if he'd been in my shoes he would have been in the pub all week.

• • •

With the Premier League title ceremony to come, our wedding in three weeks' time, Euro 2016 little more than a month away and a couple of individual awards to collect, so much was going on that it was hard to keep up. I was named the Premier League Player of the Year on Friday that week, and the evening before I went to London with Becky to pick up the Football Writers' Association Footballer of the Year award, which was a huge honour.

We've had our fair share of run-ins with the media, usually involving articles nowhere near the sports pages, and I alluded to a few of those issues in my speech that night when I said how 'it had been explained to me a few times that I needed to make a distinction between football reporters and those who don't have a clue about the game ... although I'm still slightly confused by that, given that a lot of people in this room tipped Leicester to be relegated this season!'

It was an occasion that we both really enjoyed. The Football Writers' Association really looked after us, and it's an amazing award to pick up, especially when you look through the previous winners, people like Sir Stanley Matthews, Bobby Moore, George Best, Eric Cantona, Dennis Bergkamp and

Cristiano Ronaldo, and realise that your name is going to be on that list.

We travelled back from London late that night, and I couldn't wait to get back on the pitch. I hadn't kicked a ball in anger for the best part of three weeks, so Everton on Saturday couldn't come quickly enough, especially as that was when we were going to be presented with the Premier League trophy.

It was also our final home match of the season, and everything was handled with a touch of class, starting with Italian tenor Andrea Bocelli's spine-tingling performance. He came into the dressing room before the game and Claudio introduced us one by one. I shook hands with Andrea and he said to me, 'Oh, Mr Vardy. You are a legend in Italy.' It was a lovely thing to say and it made me smile. We had our photo taken together afterwards, along with his son.

We didn't get to see Andrea singing on the pitch, because when he walked out that was our cue to finish the warm-up and head back inside. But you could hear him when we were in the dressing room. It was fantastic. Usually, you don't want anything to take your focus away from a match, but that was sensational. I made a point of watching it back a few days later, just because I wanted to actually see him singing. There he was on a stage with just a microphone, in a huge stadium, and it looked so effortless. I liked how he changed 'Time to Say Goodbye' to 'Time to Win Again', and there was that little glance with a smile at Claudio standing next to him. Claudio looked so proud.

I could feel the weight of the occasion when we walked out onto the pitch before kick-off, but it was only going to inspire us because we were so focused on playing like champions. Kingy, the sole survivor from the Leicester team that won promotion from League One, was outstanding that day. He set up my opening goal, scored the second and was named man of the match. It was typical Kingy – he never lets you down.

I got my second goal, and twenty-fourth of the season, from the penalty spot after Joel Robles, the Everton keeper, tried to play mind games. 'You're going to go down the middle', he said to me as I put it on the spot, bringing back memories of my conversation with the keeper in that penalty shootout with Stocksbridge all those years ago. I told him that I wouldn't, struck it to his right and, sure enough, he stayed in the middle. But I didn't look so clever with my next penalty kick, when I tried to burst the net for what would have been my first Premier League hat-trick and nearly hit the helicopter circling the stadium instead.

All the fans were chanting for Kasper when I took the penalty, but I didn't really understand why. Afterwards, I spoke to Peter Schmeichel, the legendary Man United keeper and Kasper's dad, and he said that his only career goal in England was against Everton, so I regretted not stepping aside and letting Kasper take it. He'd almost certainly have done a better job than me.

We outplayed Everton and won 3–1, which felt like a fitting way to sign off before the presentation ceremony. While we were waiting in the dressing room after the final whistle, I couldn't wait to get back out on the pitch. I'd watched this sort of occasion on TV when I was growing up, when the Premier League trophy seemed to belong to Manchester United and you'd see legends of the game picking up another winners' medal. Now it was our turn – Leicester City – and nobody could say that we didn't deserve it.

We walked out one by one, with the staff lined up on the right-hand side of the pitch, together with Vichai and Top, to shake hands with each of us en route to the stage. It was an amazing scene, with the fans waving their flags and 'Championes' ringing out.

We each picked up our medals, and then I was bouncing up and down on the stage, holding onto Claudio's shoulders as we waited for the trophy. He looked around to see who it was, but he probably knew without turning his head, especially if he was tuned into the right frequency.

Wes stepped forward and stood alongside Claudio to receive the trophy, it was such a special moment. For a second or two Wes paused and looked up at the sky – I think he wanted to savour what was about to happen – and then it was like the party at my house all over again, only this time we were sharing the feeling with over 30,000 fans.

It was surreal, and tempting to think that if we pinched ourselves we'd wake up. With the exception of Huthy, who'd won the title twice as a youngster with Chelsea, I don't think any of us ever expected to be in a position where we'd have a Premier League winners' medal draped around our necks.

Nearly all of us in that team had suffered rejection at one stage or another, quite a few had played lower league football and, let's be honest, clubs like Leicester aren't supposed to win the title. I think that's why everyone found our story so inspirational, not just in terms of football or sport, but more generally. It shows that anything's possible in life if you get the right group of people together.

There I was at the age of 29, after spending almost a decade in non-league football, holding the Premier League trophy above my head. It proves what you can achieve if you put your mind to it.

Becky and the children were there to enjoy that moment, as were the Inbetweeners, who'd made their regular trip down from Sheffield to be part of an occasion they could never have imagined when they were getting on a minibus to Halifax or Fleetwood to watch me play.

It was a day that put a smile on the face of so many people, and my phone was full of congratulatory text messages, including one from Serge Pizzorno, the guitarist in Kasabian, who's a lifelong Leicester supporter and someone I'd got to know well. It simply said: 'Thank you for the days, brother'.

We still had one fixture to go, which was a trip to Stamford Bridge, where the Chelsea players lined up on the pitch to form a guard of honour. One man deserved that gesture more than anyone else, and that was Claudio, who was returning to his former club. He received a tremendous ovation from everyone connected with Chelsea, and Eden Hazard was pretty popular with our supporters, too. 'Eden Hazard, he's one of our own', sang the travelling fans, who were still in party mode.

I didn't get the goal that I needed to share the golden boot with Harry Kane, but that didn't bother me in the slightest. We were Premier League champions, that's all that mattered, and finishing the season with a positive result, which we got courtesy of Drinky's 25-yard strike, was more than enough.

Twenty-four hours later we travelled from London to Leicester for the open-top bus parade, and it was another extraordinary day. Our supporters had been tremendous all season, but to see that many people – almost 250,000 – across all generations lining the streets as the bus weaved its way through the city centre really brought home the significance of what we'd achieved.

There were fans leaning out of windows, standing on the top of phone boxes and climbing up lamp posts – one guy even found a vantage point where he could shower us in champagne. Someone threw me a can of beer, which I wasn't going to waste, and I was also handed a 'Chat Shit, Get Banged' T-shirt that I put on for a minute or so, thinking that it was probably the only time that I would get away with wearing it on official Leicester duty.

Neil Plumb, the club photographer, made the fatal mistake of leaving his camera unattended for a moment on the open-top bus, so I picked it up and had some fun taking pictures of anything and everything.

Yet the image of the day was captured in my mind and will stay there for ever. We got off the bus at Victoria Park, where we were each introduced on stage, and none of us were prepared for the sight that greeted us: tens of thousands of blue-and-white shirts and flags stretched out into the distance, as far as the eye could see. It just blew me away. That was the moment when I realised we'd created memories that would last a lifetime, for them and for us, and for a city and a football club that would never be the same again.

EPILOGUE

Six weeks exactly. From that amazing sunlit evening in Victoria Park to the nightmare that was the Stade de Nice in France. Even fairytale endings have their limits.

Some setbacks are much harder to accept than others, and it will be a long time before I put the European Championship finals in France behind me. The goal I came off the bench to hook home against Wales should go down as a career highlight – scoring for your country in a major tournament is what you dream about doing as a child.

Yet everything was tarnished by our defeat in the knock-out stage, so it's hard for me to think about anything that happened in France with any fondness. The Iceland match was just horrible – my worst experience in football, bar none. At the final whistle I felt absolutely empty, and I shared the pain of every England supporter. I'm an England fan too and always will be, whether I'm playing for them or not.

I don't have the answers to where it all went wrong. All I know is that it was unbearable to be in the dressing room afterwards knowing that we'd let everyone down, and hearing Roy, who'd given me my chance to play for England, say that he was resigning.

• • •

It was a turbulent few weeks, all in all, because Arsenal also triggered the release clause in my Leicester contract on the eve of the Euros, giving me a huge decision to make. There was so much to consider as I tried to work out the pros and cons.

With people like Alexis Sanchez and Mesut Özil creating chances, Arsenal felt that they could benefit me as much as I could benefit them. I could see that, but I also thought about the tactical aspect. You look at Arsenal's style of play, and they don't get the ball forward quickly in the same way that Leicester do for those runs that I like to make in behind the defence.

One thing that didn't worry me was the idea that I wouldn't be the 'main man' at Arsenal. Every time I've moved I've managed to meet the challenge in front of me, and I'd have backed myself to do that at Arsenal.

It's a measure of how seriously we were weighing things up that we looked at new schools for the children, but I got to the stage where I felt with my heart and my head that I wanted to stay at Leicester. It wasn't to do with 'loyalty' or how I feel about my teammates, because as much as I think of those lads, players will always come and go in football. It was more a case of seeing Leicester as a club that want to build on what we achieved with the Premier League title – and I want to be part of that. I've signed a new contract, which gives four years' security for my family as well, so I'm happy with how everything has turned out. 'The dream continues', Claudio texted me after I agreed to stay, and that's exactly how I felt.

* * *

I've had my foot pressed hard against the accelerator for a while, yet even by my standards the summer of 2016 was full on. Sometimes it feels like there's no middle ground. Then again, maybe I wouldn't want any. I don't do half measures, on or off the pitch. It's all or nothing, and that's always been my approach to life.

It's been a help at times and a hindrance on other occasions, but those close to me accept me for what I am. I know I've made a few mistakes along the way, but so have other people when it comes to me. It turned out that I wasn't too small to be a professional footballer, and I did have the potential that others couldn't see.

I was heartbroken when Wednesday released me, and it wasn't as if I sat down and navigated a way back – most people would have picked a quicker route than climbing every rung of the non-league ladder via Stocksbridge Park Steels, Halifax and Fleetwood. I didn't give up on the dream during that period, but I wasn't chasing it either. I can't ever remember clocking on at the factory and thinking about being a Premier League footballer or lining up for England one day. Most of the time I was just hoping that someone had brought a ball in with them so we could have a kickabout during our lunch-break – and I was still doing that at the age of 24.

Five years later I had a Premier League winners' medal around my neck, Ruud van Nistelrooy was poking his head around the door of the England dressing room to say hello, a screenwriter was sitting across the table discussing a Hollywood movie and there was a trophy on my mantelpiece that Eden Hazard, Luis Suárez and Gareth Bale had won in each of the previous three seasons. It's madness, and I struggle to believe what has happened as much as anybody else.

My ability was definitely always there, but the dedication wasn't, certainly not after Wednesday let me go and I lost my way. Playing non-league brought me back, and signing for Leicester was the making of me. Yet it could easily have broken me, too. I'll always look back on that conversation with Nigel Pearson, Steve Walsh and Craig Shakespeare during my first season at the club, when I was at rock bottom, as a career-defining moment. I was ready to walk away from it all then.

Instead, Nigel and his staff made me believe that I could play at that level.

Becky was the person who brought some calm to the chaos and allowed me to turn my life around off the field. Her support has enabled me to focus on football in a way that I never did before.

Don't get me wrong, I've not suddenly become a little angel. I still enjoy a couple of beers and the dressing room will never be a quiet place with me around, but I've definitely calmed down. The Soar Point hasn't seen me for a few years now, and the old Jamie Vardy wouldn't have been tucked up in bed at half-past eight the night before his wedding. I'd probably have got carried away like one of the ushers, necked a bottle of tequila and ended up on a drip in hospital. Only Gary Taylor-Fletcher, my former Leicester teammate, can explain what he was thinking there, other than to give everyone a load of ammunition for the speeches.

Our wedding was a perfect day at Peckforton Castle, shared with so many good friends, and there was even a rare glimpse of emotion from me when Sofia, our daughter, tiptoed down the aisle moments before Becky. As I looked at her little face, I welled up. That's what family life has come to mean to me.

The children help to keep everything in perspective, which allows me to handle the ups and downs of football in a way that

I couldn't a few years ago, when every win or defeat got washed down with a glass of Skittle vodka or something stronger.

We went on holiday to Portugal later in the summer, and as I sat on the back of a little fishing boat with the children, catching nothing but the sunshine and looking forward to the arrival of a new baby, I couldn't have been in a happier place.

* * *

I'm excited about the next chapter of my career. I might be 29 but I've only been a professional footballer for 4 years, so my legs have got plenty of running left in them yet.

I also launched the V9 Academy over the summer of 2016 with one eye on the future. I want to help players who find themselves in a similar position to the one I was in during my non-league days, so I'm running an annual five-day residential course in Manchester, where players from lower down the pyramid will have the chance to perform in front of professional clubs, starting in May 2017. It would be brilliant if we could give a few lads a route into the Football League and the opportunity to follow in my footsteps.

It's so tough trying to break into the professional game, especially if your confidence has taken a knock through being told you haven't got what it takes. I know exactly what that feels like, and it's even harder to accept when you've devoted years and years of your life to trying to make it somewhere, because at the end of it you feel as though you've lost your childhood as well as your football club.

I've proved people wrong in that sense, but it wasn't my main motivation. I just wanted to enjoy kicking a ball again, and Stocksbridge gave me that chance. It was a hell of a long road back from there, but I wouldn't change a thing. That hunger, passion and desire that I take onto the pitch with me is a product of where I've come from, and I hope my experiences can inspire others to believe that rejection can be a start, not the end, of your journey.

ACKNOWLEDGEMENTS

Working on this book has reminded me just how far I've come and what an amazing journey it's been. Trying to piece everything together has taken up a lot of time, but I've really enjoyed the experience. It's evoked so many memories – in some cases with a bit of prodding from friends. Ashley Cross, who worked with me at the Trulife factory, and Brett Lovell, my old Stocksbridge Park Steels teammate, I owe you both a beer for your help.

People flit in and out of your life in the football world, where everything changes so fast, but many of my managers have left a lasting impression and I'd like to take this opportunity to thank them. Gary Marrow, who was in charge at Stocksbridge Park Steels, Neil Aspin, who signed me for FC Halifax Town, Micky Mellon who managed me at Fleetwood Town and, of course, Nigel Pearson and Claudio Ranieri at Leicester – you all believed in me and I'll always be grateful.

When I think about players whose company I've enjoyed on and off the pitch, there are far too many to mention. But I do feel a special debt of gratitude to my teammates at Leicester, in particular the group that wrote their names into the history books by winning the Premier League title. I know that any personal success I achieved across that period wouldn't have been possible without those players.

I also want to thank Dave Rennie, the Leicester physio, for running his eyes over the sections in the book relating to my injuries – and for patching me up from time to time. Thanks to all the other staff at the club who've helped me across my time at Leicester, especially Craig Shakespeare, Claudio's assistant, and Steve Walsh, who has now moved on.

My agent John Morris has been with me since 2011, back when I was playing non-league football, and his support, advice and encouragement has been invaluable over the years. Thanks to John and his colleagues at Key Sports.

In putting this book together, I'd like to thank Stuart James for all his hard work and dedication and to everyone at Ebury for their commitment, but in particular to Andrew Goodfellow and Laura Horsley, who were so enthusiastic about my story.

Most importantly of all, thanks to my wife Becky and the children. Your love and support means so much to me. Everything that I do on the pitch is for you.